Until it was Real

THE RAIDER BROTHERS

D. E. Haggerty

Also by D.E. Haggerty

Bragg's Love
Perfect Bragg
Bragg's Match
Bragg's Christmas
A Hero for Hailey
A Protector for Phoebe
A Soldier for Suzie
A Fox for Faith
A Christmas for Chrissie
A Valentine for Valerie
A Love for Lexi
About Face
At Arm's Length
Hands Off
Knee Deep
Molly's Misadventures

Chapter 1

Dakota – a woman who won't let a little thing like women dressed as mermaids stop her

DAKOTA

I'm driving onto the bridge connecting the mainland to the island of Smuggler's Hideaway when the car engine makes a weird knocking noise.

"Come on, Matilda. We're almost there. No giving up now."

Matilda's engine continues to make an awful racket as I drive over the bridge. By the time the tires hit solid ground, my hands are clenching the steering wheel, and my heart is racing. Phew. I made it.

To my relief, the car keeps chugging away, and I follow the directions I memorized before beginning this journey – Matilda doesn't believe in GPS – and arrive at the *Mermaid Motel* five minutes later. I'm surprised the parking lot is packed. I drive around until I manage to snag a spot in the back of the lot.

I switch Matilda off, but her engine knocks and rattles a few more times before giving up. I hope she'll start on Monday. I don't fancy the idea of hiking to *Buccaneer's Whiskey & Distillery* in my heels and work clothes. Especially since my one nice pair of shoes needs to last as long as possible.

I climb out of the car and stretch my sore limbs. I've been sitting for entirely too long. Matilda didn't want to start at the last gas station I stopped at and, once I got a kind trucker to jump the car, I didn't want to chance stopping again.

I grab my purse and shut the door. The hinges scream, but the door stops before it's shut. I push it again, but it doesn't budge.

"Matilda," I mutter as I slam my hip against the door. The door clicks shut, and I rub a hand over my hip. Ouch. Note to self: the car is stronger than my hip.

I make my way through the parking lot toward the reception.

"Hi," I greet the woman behind the desk. "I'm Dakota. I'm checking—"

"Thank the smugglers!" she shouts as she throws her arms in the air. "I tried to call you to make sure you were still arriving today but when you didn't answer I panicked. Our night manager ran off with a mermaid, so I'm afraid you need to start working tonight instead of next week. I hope that's okay."

I blink. "Your night manager ran off with a mermaid?"

She groans. "It happens every year. I need to stop hiring men. They're weak."

Her response did not clear up my confusion one bit. "Did you say mermaid?"

She rolls her eyes. "They overtake the island this time of year."

I scratch my neck. "Is mermaid code for another word?"

She bursts into laughter. "I forgot you're not from the island. The look on your face."

I'm certain my face still appears confused since her laughter is not helping the situation. What have I done? Why am I here?

Freaking Adam. This is all his fault. If my husband wasn't already dead, I'd wring his neck for putting me in this position. I can't believe how thoroughly and completely he fooled me.

She holds out her hand. "I'm Sadie. Welcome to Smuggler's Hideaway."

"Dakota," I say as we shake hands.

"A quick rundown. Smugglers are sexy. Mermaids are real. And seals are wild animals. They shouldn't be touched."

"O-o-o-kay?"

I must be dreaming. Smugglers, mermaids, seals?

Did I fall asleep driving? Or maybe Matilda is leaking carbon monoxide, and I'm slowly being poisoned. I hope I didn't throw up in the car. I'll never get the smell out.

"Shoot a smuggler," Sadie mutters. "It was too much, too fast, wasn't it? My sisters are always saying I need to explain myself better. Let me try again." She straightens her shoulders. "Welcome to the island, Dakota. Mermaids are real."

She motions to a group of women exiting the elevator. They're dressed up as mermaids, complete with seashell bras and shimmery skirts shaped like fins.

"Why are they…" I trail off as they pass us, chattering away.

"This is beyond exciting."

"I can't believe they dropped the kiss rule."

"I love it. We can vote for whoever we want as the sexiest man on the island."

"Vote for whoever you want. I'm winning the auction."

The door slams behind them and it's quiet once again in the reception area. I return my attention to Sadie.

"I think I made a mistake."

She shackles my wrist before I can escape. "No, please, don't go. I can't work another twenty-four-hour shift. I need sleep. Sleep is my friend. Sleep is good."

She has no reason to worry. I might have made a mistake, but I'm not going anywhere. Because I have nowhere to go. And I need money. Lots and lots of money. Thus, a job at the motel *and* a job at the local whiskey distillery.

But – despite copious amounts of evidence to the contrary – I'm not a pushover. And I can recognize an opportunity when it knocks on my door.

"Let's talk terms."

"I'll raise your salary by 10 percent." When I don't respond, she rushes on. "And I'll give you the honeymoon suite to stay in."

"The honeymoon suite?"

I don't want to know what the honeymoon suite looks like on an island where women dress up as mermaids and discuss kissing rules as if they're normal.

"Okay. Fine. The owner's suite."

I tap my chin and feign considering her offer when in reality, my heart is trying to beat its way out of my chest. I had resigned myself to living in a dingy hotel room for the rest of my life. The owner's suite has got to be better. Plus, a ten percent raise. Eek!

I hold out my hand. "I'll take it."

"You had me worried there, Dakota."

"We're even since I thought I was having a stroke with all this talk of mermaids."

She giggles. "You're going to love Smuggler's Hideaway."

She sets a 'Be Right Back' sign on the desk. "Come on. Let me show you to your suite."

I follow her out the door and to the left. The *Mermaid Motel* is set up in a classic motel style with all of the doors to the rooms facing the parking lot. I'd prefer a hotel with a corridor, but beggars can't be choosers.

"The owners don't live in the owner's apartment?" I ask.

"The owners don't live on the island. I've never met them in person," Sadie says as she opens the door to the suite. "Ta da!"

I glance around. There's a small kitchen to my left, and straight ahead is a living room with a sofa and a television. The furniture is a bit dated but otherwise it seems fine. Better than what I expected.

"The microwave works, but I wouldn't use the oven. The last time I tried heating a pizza in there, I set off the smoke alarm." Sadie continues the tour. "The television works, but if you want to watch anything besides the local channels, you'll need to sign up for a streaming service."

I doubt I'll have any time for watching television, considering I'll be working two full-time jobs, but I keep quiet. If she knows I have another job, she might not be so keen on keeping me on as the night manager.

She opens the door to the separate bedroom. "You don't get housekeeping service, but they'll wash your linens and towels."

The bedroom is small. The only furniture is a double bed and a dresser against the opposite wall. The bedspread is an ugly brown but I have my sheets and comforter in the car. Besides some of my clothes, the bedding is one of the few items I was able to save from my old life. No one wants to buy used bedding apparently.

"There's a closet here, and your bathroom is here." Sadie points to the bathroom door. "I'd stay away from the bathtub. The last time I used it, it leaked water everywhere."

Between the bathtub and oven, I'm wondering if the owner's suite was such a good idea. Maybe I'd be better off with a regular motel room. Although, I haven't been in one of the motel rooms yet.

"No bathtub. No oven. Got it."

"Do you want me to help you with your luggage?" she asks when we return to the living room.

"No, thanks. I don't have much." I hold my breath as I wait for her response. I don't want Sadie to see how pathetic my car is.

After my previous car – I loved my little Fiat 500 – was repossessed, I had to scramble to buy another car. I didn't have much cash, and my credit score is scary bad after all the shenanigans Adam pulled.

Did he think I'd never learn the truth? I nearly snort. He probably thought he'd live forever. A car accident ended those delusions of grandeur.

"Here are your keys."

I shove them into my pocket and head for the door.

"What?" I ask Sadie when she doesn't follow.

"Um. I wasn't kidding about our previous night manager running off with a mermaid. I know you're not supposed to start until next week, but if you could work tonight, you'd be a life saver."

I have no desire to stay up all night working after driving for the past three days, but I need the money.

"It's fine. I can work tonight. Once I've brought my things inside, I'll join you at the desk and you can go through my tasks with me."

"Woo-hoo!" she shouts. "Thank the singing mermaids!"

"Or you could just thank me."

She throws an arm over my shoulders. "We're going to be great friends, Dakota. I can tell."

I hope so. I could use a friend after the way my friends dumped me once the truth about Adam came out.

Maybe moving to Smuggler's Hideaway won't be so bad after all.

We exit the apartment and a woman dressed as a mermaid nearly runs into me. The man chasing her catches up to her and throws her over his shoulder. "You've been a bad mermaid. I need to punish you."

She giggles as he carries her away.

I change my mind. Smuggler's Hideaway is going to take some getting used to.

Chapter 2

Rhett – a man who wishes he could strangle his brothers without his mother finding out

RHETT

I slap the switch to turn on the lights when I enter *Buccaneer's Whiskey & Distillery*. Despite being thirty minutes late, I'm the first one to arrive at the offices. My brothers and punctuality do not go together. Whose bright idea was it for the six of us to own a business together?

Oh, right, it was Eli's. Easy enough for my oldest brother. He lives in California for the most part. He doesn't have to try and wrangle our brothers into behaving on a daily basis.

Except Eli is returning home next week and he claims he's going to stay. I'm not certain I believe him. He hightailed it out of Smuggler's Hideaway for college and has barely returned since.

I pass the offices of my brothers Miles and Zane. Both are empty. No surprise there. I keep going until I reach the door to the distillery. My two other brothers, Kai and Jaxon, should be in here.

I locate Jaxon in his lab. He doesn't bother to look up from labeling the small bottles filled with whiskey samples when I enter.

"Jaxon," I call.

"Busy."

"Is Kai in yet?"

"I am not Kai's keeper."

I sigh. I don't know why I bothered to ask. Jaxon lives in his own world as the master distiller. I'd complain about him being anti-social but this is just the way he is. His concentration skills are legendary. Anyone who can manage to study for a physics test while his three younger brothers wrestle on the ground in front of him has my admiration.

I don't bother to say goodbye as I leave and go in search of Kai. Kai is the operations manager for *Buccaneer's Whiskey* and should be here to manage the logistical and organizational aspects of the distillery.

I fought Eli long and hard when he appointed Kai as the operations manager. Kai is the youngest of the Raider brothers and he believes being on time is for boring old men.

But my oldest brother wouldn't change his mind. He wanted all of the management roles for the distillery – *our* distillery, according to him – to be filled by his brothers. And since Zane is a marketing whizz, Jaxon is a scientific genius, and I'm the numbers guy, there was no one left.

Except Miles. But he flat out refused to accept the position. He told Eli he didn't want any part of the distillery. He's the sales manager *when* he deigns to come into the office. He can usually be found in the ocean on his surfboard.

I'm not surprised when I can't locate Kai anywhere in the distillery. I return to the offices and nearly bump into Zane.

"You're here."

"Where else would I be?"

Who knows? Zane could literally be up to anything from hitchhiking across South America to holed up in a kibbutz in Israel when he's not at work. He's a free spirit who's determined to try everything at least once in his life.

"I need your help."

He holds up his hands. "Dude. If I've told you once, I've told you twice, I am not checking your junk for signs of an STD."

I glare at him. "I do not have an STD."

Zane snorts. "What about the time you got dots on your junk and were convinced you had genital measles?"

"Genital measles isn't a thing."

"Which is what we told you at the time."

"You shouldn't have crept into my room and drawn dots all over me."

"It wasn't me. Kai did it."

"I deny all responsibility," Kai says as he strolls into the building. "Unless it was awesome, in which case, it was probably me."

"Good. You're here. I need your help."

Kai rolls back on his heels. "It's good you finally recognize your limitations, old man. But I am not helping you go to the toilet."

"I am not an old man," I grumble. "And I don't need any fucking help going to the toilet."

"Good. I should probably get to work."

I shackle his wrist before he can escape. "I need your help bringing some furniture inside."

From the corner of my eye, I catch Zane trying to sneak off. "You too," I bark at him.

His shoulders slump. "Moving furniture is boring."

"Boring is not being able to travel because your car doesn't work."

He narrows his eyes on me. "You wouldn't dare pour sugar in my gas tank again. I'll tell Mom."

I shrug. "Tell Mom what you want. Let's find out who she believes." Since Zane thinks telling lies is fun, Mom hardly ever believes him – even when he's telling the truth. "Or you can help me move some furniture and we can get back to work."

"You're going the wrong way," Miles says as I walk outside with Kai and Zane on my heels.

"We're moving furniture," Zane says with a distinct pout in his voice.

"What furniture?" Miles asks as he follows us to my SUV.

"It's not much. A desk, chair, and filing cabinet."

"If you're getting a new chair, I want a new chair," Kai says.

"You're not getting a new chair until you apologize for what you did to mine," I say.

"No one touched your chair," he claims.

I fist my hands on my hips. "It got shorter and shorter every day on its own?"

I seriously thought I was losing my mind until I examined the bottom of the chair and realized someone was messing with the settings. My money's on Kai.

Zane shrugs. "Maybe you've been gaining weight and the chair couldn't handle it."

I grunt. "I haven't been gaining weight."

Kai sighs. "It's normal to gain weight as you get old."

"I'm not fucking old just because you're a baby."

"I'm not a baby."

Miles clears his throat. "Technically, you are the baby of the family."

"I'll show you baby." Kai flies at Miles and tackles him to the ground.

"I don't have time for this shit," I mumble as I grab both of them by the back of their t-shirts and shake them. "Enough or I'll tell Mom."

"Tattletale," Kai snarls as he yanks away from me.

"I wouldn't have to tattletale if you'd just listen to me."

"Why should we listen to you?" Miles asks. "You're not the boss of us."

I rub my neck, but it doesn't relieve any of the tension building there. My brothers all love to remind me how I'm not their boss. I'm not their dad. I'm not their parent. The list goes on and on.

But who was the person who made sure they finished their homework every night? Who made sure they made it to school every day? Who made sure they got to sports practice every afternoon?

It sure as hell wasn't our dad since he took off when I was fifteen and never looked back. And it wasn't our mom. Don't get me wrong. She did the best she could. She worked two jobs to give us a roof over our heads and provide food on the table.

But when she wasn't working, she was falling apart. Dad's leaving broke something in her. Something that couldn't be fixed until Stuart entered our lives.

And it wasn't my big brother Eli. Eli did his thing. He worked two or three jobs to make sure my brothers and I could buy new clothes and join sports teams, and have a bit of extra money to go out on a date. But he wasn't there every day. I was.

And I've been listening to my brothers bitch about me ever since.

"The furniture is for Eli's new assistant. She's starting tomorrow," I explain, since trying to talk sense into my brothers is a waste of time and effort.

Miles rubs his hands together. "I hope she's sexy and wears tight skirts and high heels."

I slap him upside the head. "You are not going to seduce Eli's assistant."

He widens his eyes and feigns innocence. "I don't seduce women. I can't help it if they fall into my lap."

"None of you." I glare at them. "Is going to seduce or date or flirt or whatever you want to call it with Eli's new assistant."

Zane's nose wrinkles. "Whatever we want to call it? Are you having memory problems?"

I swear, if Mom wouldn't haunt me, I'd strangle my brother. Having siblings is a pain in my ass.

"Mom should have stopped having children after me," I mutter as I open the door of my SUV and start pulling boxes out.

"Don't be jealous, Mom loves me more than you," Kai says as he picks up a box and carries it away.

"Mom loves all of us equally," Miles hollers after him.

"I'm the favorite," Zane claims.

I ignore them as we carry the boxes into the office side of the distillery building.

"You're welcome!" Kai shouts as he drops his load in the empty reception area and walks away.

"Where do you think you're going?"

He taps his empty wrist. "Need to get to work. Don't want to anger the boss."

"Me too," Miles says as he aims for the door.

"Your office is in the other direction."

"Dude, the waves are calling my name."

I bite my tongue before I lash out at him. Eli hired Miles knowing he didn't want anything to do with the distillery. I can threaten to fire him all I want. He doesn't care. He doesn't want or need the money from this job. All he needs is a surfboard and the ocean. If he hadn't injured his shoulder a while back, he'd be a pro surfer.

Zane sighs. "I'll help."

I shoo him away. "Not after the last time you 'helped' put a bed together and Miles ended up with a concussion when it collapsed."

"It's not my fault he was jumping on it."

"Except you dared him to use the bed as a springboard to fly out of the window."

"He didn't have to accept the dare."

None of my brothers can refuse a dare. It's why I know the ER doctor by her first name and am intimately acquainted with the jail cells on Smuggler's Hideaway.

"Go. I've got this."

He ambles away and I open the first box and get to work. The way I always do. I'm always the one taking care of my brothers. And I always will be.

Eli returning home won't change a thing.

Chapter 3

"Who pissed in your Cheerios?" ~ Dakota

DAKOTA

Knock! Knock! Knock!

Huh. What's going on? Why is someone knocking on my door? I hope there's not an emergency in the motel. It was bad enough I spent half the night listening to a drunk mermaid complain about how all the good smugglers were taken.

I probably should have researched Smuggler's Hideaway before I decided to upend my entire life to the island. Although, my entire life went up in flames after my husband's funeral anyway. There wasn't much to salvage from the ashes.

"Get out of here!"

My eyes fly open, and I look to my side to discover a large man looming toward me. "AARGH!"

"What are you screaming about?"

I clutch my chest as I scan the area. What in the world is going on? With a start, I realize I'm in my car. I glance down at myself and notice I'm dressed for work at the distillery.

I must not be dreaming since I tend to be naked in my dreams. And I don't care what anyone says. Dreaming I'm naked does not mean I'm sexually repressed.

"Come on." The man knocks on my car window again. "Move it along. This isn't a parking spot for vagrants."

Vagrants. I'm not a vagrant. Is he an idiot?

I open the door and he jumps away before I hit him.

"What are you doing? There's no reason to get out of your car. Drive away. We don't have a restroom or shower for you to use."

My nostrils flare at his words. "I don't need a restroom or shower, Mr. High and Mighty."

A muscle ticks in his jaw at my words, and try as I might, I can't miss how sexy the move is. And those eyes that are glaring at me are pretty darn sexy, too. They're a deep blue a woman could drown in.

"My name is not Mr. High and Mighty," he growls and my stomach dips. Someone has a deep, growly voice I wouldn't mind hearing growl my name in my ear.

"Sorry. Do you prefer I refer to you as jerk?"

He fists his hands at his side and I notice how big they are. I bet those hands are strong enough to lift me up and place me on the nearest flat surface. Considering how tall he is, it would have to be a high surface for our parts to line up.

"Are you listening to me? We don't allow vagrants to park here."

All visions of us getting horizontal disappear. I spit daggers out of my eyes at him.

"I am not a vagrant."

He motions to my car. "Could have fooled me."

I nearly cringe since my car is cringeworthy, but I don't.

"Judgy much?"

He leans forward and I tilt my head back to meet his gaze. "I'm not the one who was sleeping in their car in a parking lot."

He's also not the one who worked eight hours last night before rushing to shower and change into business attire for her first day as a personal assistant to a billionaire. The man is clueless but I'm not filling him in. Karma will take care of his ass.

I inhale a deep breath and search for calm. Mr. High and Mighty probably works at the distillery. Making an enemy of another employee on my first day is not a good idea. I want allies, not enemies.

"I was not sleeping in my car," I manage to say without gritting my teeth.

He snorts. "Liar. I literally saw you."

"I am not a liar!" So much for calm. "There's a difference between accidentally falling asleep while you wait for a business to open up and sleeping somewhere on purpose."

He rolls his eyes. "It sounds as if… Hold on. Did you say you're waiting for the business to open?"

"Yes."

"This business?" He motions to the distillery.

I spread out my arms. "I don't see any other businesses around here."

Buccaneer's Whiskey & Distillery is not located in one of the towns on Smuggler's Hideaway. It sits on its own land halfway between Smuggler's Rest where the *Mermaid Motel* is and Rogue's Landing. The other town on the island is Pirate's Perch, but I haven't had time to visit it yet.

"Why are you…" He trails off and swears under his breath. "You're Dakota."

I hold out my hand. "Dakota Bell."

I don't add how it's nice to meet him because – despite what he thinks – I'm not a liar.

He shakes my hand and I nearly jolt when I feel a spark of electricity. His eyes widen and he drops my hand. I guess he feels it, too. And, guessing by how quickly he dropped my hand, he's not happy about it.

I get it, Mr. High and Mighty. I don't want to be attracted to you either. Even though I'm happy to discover my libido didn't die with my husband.

"Rhett Raider," he grumbles.

Raider? As in one of the founding brothers of the distillery? Well, shit. This day just went from bad to worse, and the clock hasn't struck nine yet.

"Eli told me you'd be starting today. I'll show you around."

He pivots and marches to the building. I grab my purse and slam my car door shut before rushing after him. By the time we reach the building, I'm gasping for air.

"If I had known about today's race, I wouldn't have worn heels," I mutter.

Rhett's gaze drops to my feet. His appraising look has me wanting to squirm. I lock my muscles before he notices the effect on me. This is my new boss's brother. And he's a jerk. My body is confused because it's not used to getting any attention from men, is all.

"We're pretty casual here." He unlocks the door and motions me inside.

Casual? He's wearing a pair of khakis with a button-down shirt. And Eli was wearing a three-piece suit when he interviewed me. Granted, he was at his office in California, but still, I wasn't going to show up wearing a sundress. Not on my first day at least.

"This is your work area."

I glance around the room. It's basically the foyer but there's a decent-sized workstation set up in one corner.

He points to a piece of paper on the desk. "Your username, password, and keys to the building."

I set my purse down and reach for the piece of paper.

Rhett clears his throat. "I'll show you the rest of the offices and the distillery and then you can get settled. Eli said he'd email you a list of things he needs you to do since he's still in California until next week."

"Okay."

I follow him down a corridor of offices. "This is Eli's office. I'm next door. Zane and Miles are across the hallway."

"What is your position? And what do Zane and Miles do?"

"As little as possible," he mutters before raising his voice. "I'm the CFO. Zane is Head of Marketing and Miles is Head of Sales."

The corridor ends at an industrial sized door. "This is the entrance to the distillery. You probably won't need to go in here often."

"Okay."

"Jaxon will give you a tour if you want one."

Of course, I want one. I technically work for Eli and not the distillery. But I'll be working here at the distillery every day. I want to know everything about it. Making whiskey sounds way more interesting than plumbing, which is where I worked before.

"I'll ask him when I meet him."

"Good luck with him. He's a bit shy."

I flash a smile at Rhett. "Don't worry. I'll charm him."

He scowls. "No charming my brothers. This is a work environment. Not the chance for you to bag a millionaire."

I whip out a salute. "Aye, Aye, Captain High and Mighty."

"And stop calling me High and Mighty."

If the shoe fits…

The door to the offices bangs open and a man strolls inside. "Who's High and Mighty?"

Rhett scowls. "This is my brother, Zane."

I shake his hand. "Marketing, isn't it?"

"Marketing, fun maker, I can be whatever you need." He winks.

Rhett growls. "I told you. No flirting with Eli's PA."

Zane widens his eyes and feigns innocence. I met the man two seconds ago, and even I know he's the furthest thing from innocent. I recognize a troublemaker when I meet one.

I roll my eyes. "Mr. High and Mighty doesn't approve of fun."

Zane chuckles. "I love you already."

I relax. I was worried I made the wrong decision to relocate my entire life to Smuggler's Hideaway when I met Rhett, but Zane is fun. As long as I don't let him talk me into dropping my panties for him, I'll be just fine.

Zane threads his arm through mine. "Miles, Kai, and I are the fun brothers. The others?" He wrinkles his nose. "Not so much. Stick with me, kid."

Rhett elbows his way in between us. "She's supposed to be working. As are you."

Zane sniffs. "Boring." He flounces away.

Rhett glares at me, and I motion toward my desk. "I'll just …"

I hurry away. I don't need to spend any more time in his presence. My body disagrees. It thinks we should jump him like a pole and take him for a ride. My body also enjoys mixing its metaphors.

It doesn't matter what my body wants. Rhett Raider is a jerk, and I plan to stay as far away from him as possible.

While working in the same building, a few doors away from each other.

Easy peasy. I got this.

Chapter 4

RHETT

"Hey." Eli stands to greet me.

"Good to have you back."

He grins before sitting behind his desk. "It's good to be back."

"And you're back for good this time?"

"I am."

I don't know if I believe him but he's my big brother who worked three jobs in high school to make sure I had the money for a pair of cleats to run track. I'll give him a chance.

I settle in a chair in front of his desk.

"What's wrong?"

I frown. "Why do you assume there's anything wrong?"

He flicks a hand toward the door. "You locked it."

Because I don't want Dakota walking in on us. I'm not worried about my brothers. Zane and Miles aren't in yet. As usual. And Kai and Jaxon stick to the distillery and avoid the offices.

"Dakota."

He sits up. "What's wrong? Did one of our idiot brothers upset her? I told you to talk to them before she arrived."

"I did talk to them." But it didn't stop each and every one of them from spending time perched on her desk, flirting with her. Even Jaxon left the distillery to speak to her.

Eli sighs. "I'll have another word with them. I don't want them chasing her away."

I scratch my neck as I contemplate how to say the next part.

"Out with it."

I grunt. "Are you certain Dakota is the best assistant for you?"

"Why? What did she do?"

She's entirely too sexy and too much of a temptation. I want to fist her blonde, curly hair while I feast on those bowtie lips before I lay her down and explore every curve she has. And she has a lot of them. I want to watch her green eyes flare as I touch her.

My cock twitches and I clear my throat before I follow those thoughts to their logical conclusion. I'm not spending another day fighting a hard-on because of Dakota. The woman is annoying I remind my cock. It doesn't care. She's sexy. It doesn't need to know anything more.

"She was sleeping in her car."

Eli's nose wrinkles. "In her car? Is she homeless? Do we need to look into accommodations for her?"

"Accommodations for her?"

"Yea." He nods. "Somewhere for her to live."

"Wouldn't you rather fire her?"

He rears back. "Fire her for being homeless? I'm not a heartless billionaire, no matter what the press says about me."

I know he's not. As one of the founding members of *Apparoo* – a game software company – Eli has more money than he knows what to do with. Thus, him founding this distillery so all of the Raider brothers can work together and stay on the island.

I hold up a hand. "I didn't mean to insinuate you're heartless. I was trying to point out how annoying Dakota is."

"Annoying?"

"She doesn't listen when I reprimand her. She snarks back at me."

"Why have you reprimanded her? She works for me, not the distillery. If you have a problem with her work, you need to speak to me about it."

"You give her tasks related to the distillery."

"Because I'm the CEO and she's my assistant."

"I don't think she's the right person to be your assistant."

Eli scoffs. "Do you know how hard it was to find someone willing to move to Smuggler's Hideaway?"

"She has no experience as an assistant."

"She managed a plumbing business. My needs aren't much different."

"Really?" I lift a brow. "Managing a bunch of plumbers unclogging toilets is the same as managing your billionaire lifestyle?"

The door flies open, and Dakota stomps into the room. "I can't believe you."

I jump to my feet. "How did you get in here?"

"You can thank me." Zane steps into the room and bows. "A little lock can't stop me."

Dakota jiggles the keys in her hands. "And I have keys to Eli's office since I'm his assistant."

Zane frowns at her. "We agreed you'd let me accept credit for opening the door."

She snorts. "You spent five minutes fiddling with it and you still couldn't get it open."

Miles glides into the room. "Are we having a meeting? What about?"

Dakota crosses her arms over her chest and glares at me. "About how Rhett went behind my back to speak to my boss about firing me."

Miles whistles. "Dick move, dude. Dick. Move."

"Why does he want to fire you?" Zane asks.

"You heard him." Dakota motions toward me. "He thinks I'm homeless and unqualified."

"You're homeless?" Zane turns on Eli. "What the hell, bro? Are you not paying her enough?"

"I'm not homeless," Dakota says.

"Except I caught you sleeping in your car the other morning," I remind her.

Her nostrils flare. "I was exhausted. So sue me for having a lot going on in my life and falling asleep. Mr. High and Mighty strikes again."

I want to ask what she has going on. What could possibly cause her to be exhausted enough to fall asleep at 8:30 in the morning in the parking lot while waiting for me to arrive?

But I don't. I don't need to know about Dakota's life. She's a work colleague. Nothing more. Nothing less.

No matter how much I want to taste those lips. I never will. I don't do relationships. And I'm not making an exception for a colleague who drives me batty.

"Stop calling me Mr. High and Mighty," I grumble.

"Stop being all high and mighty, and I might," she fires back.

Zane grins. "This is awesome. Finally, someone is putting Rhett in his place."

I scowl at him. "In my place? What the hell are you talking about?"

He flips his hand. "You're always trying to tell us what to do. It's exhausting."

Miles elbows him. "Remember the time he tried to ground us."

"I didn't *try* to ground you. I did ground you."

Miles rolls his eyes. "Total overreaction."

"Overreaction? You put hundreds of fake spiders in the principal's office."

"Hundreds? Try thousands." Zane and Miles high-five.

I frown. "You never learn your lesson."

"I wasn't the one who needed to learn a lesson," Miles says.

"Exactly," Zane agrees. "The principal deserved it. She should have never given us detention."

"She gave you detention for getting into a fight," I remind them.

Miles scowls. "Those assholes were bullying a girl."

"At least I'm not the only one who Rhett tries to control," Dakota mutters.

"I'm not trying to control you."

"You're not? Oh, right." She snaps her fingers. "You're trying to make me look bad in front of my boss and have me fired."

Eli clears his throat. "No one is getting fired."

"Thank you, Mr. Raider."

"I told you to call me Eli."

"Thank you, Eli." Dakota smiles at him, and I bite back a growl. She shouldn't be smiling and flirting with her boss. It's unprofessional. This is why she shouldn't have been hired in the first place.

Eli claps his hands. "Now, everyone, get back to work."

"Eli," I begin but he holds up a hand.

"No. I'm not discussing firing my PA with you any further."

"But—"

"This is none of your business. My PA works for me and me alone. If you have a problem with her in the future – a real problem related to her work and not some bullshit you made up because she doesn't put up with your crap – come to me and we'll discuss it."

"Whatever," I grumble before escaping the room.

I slam my office door shut behind me before stomping to my chair and collapsing in it. Eli is going to regret his decision to keep Dakota as his PA. I don't know what's going on with her yet, but there's definitely something going on.

She drives a junkie car despite the generous salary I know Eli pays her and she's tired all the time. She's up to something, and I'm going to figure it out.

Once I reveal her secret, Eli won't hesitate to fire her.

Satisfaction fills me. Perfect plan.

Chapter 5

DAKOTA

I open my suite door and check both ways for Sadie. Once I confirm the coast is clear, I shut my door and make my way toward Main Street.

Don't get me wrong. I like Sadie. She's funny and tells the best stories. She's also bored out of her mind working at the front desk. The last time I happened past her on my way to the laundry room for clean sheets, she regaled me with a story about her brothers letting the sheep escape and causing chaos all over the island for over an hour.

I don't need another story I can't understand. What I need is some time away from the hotel. Away from work.

I haven't even had a chance to check out the town of Smuggler's Rest yet. I've been either working one of my two jobs or sleeping.

I study the town as I wander. It's adorable. I could see myself settling down here. Except I could never afford to buy a house since I have a mountain of debt to pay – courtesy of my dead husband.

I wish I could invent a time machine and go back two years to divorce the jerk before he died. Unfortunately, I didn't know he was a jerk at the time. I was the naïve fool who thought he was away on business all those weekends when he was actually gambling our money away when he wasn't spending it on booze and hookers.

I should probably consider myself lucky I didn't end up with some weird STD that causes boils on your face.

Enough of Adam. I want to enjoy my first day off in two weeks.

I notice a bakery shop up ahead – Pirates Pastries. The logo is adorable – a pirate ship with a rolling pin as the steering wheel and a cupcake on the black mast. I can't not go inside now.

The place smells of sugar and coffee and chocolate. Heaven.

"Dakota Bell," a woman says when I approach the counter. "It's about time you showed up."

"Um… How do you know my name?"

She rolls her eyes. "This is Smuggler's Hideaway. Everyone knows everything."

Gosh. I hope not. I don't want to run away with my tail tucked between my legs when everyone realizes what a douchebag my dead husband was.

"I don't know who you are."

She grins. "Sassy. I like it. I'm Parker. Welcome to my bakery."

"You're a baker?" She nods. "Cool. I can't bake. It's not my fault, though. Mixers tend to go crazy when I'm in the vicinity."

She giggles. "I'm happy to fulfill your baked good needs." She motions to the display case. "Pick what you want. On the house."

"I can pay." I'm not destitute. Yet.

"It's my welcome to Smuggler's Hideaway present. Besides, once you've had one of my treats, you'll come back." She winks.

My nose wrinkles. "I probably shouldn't. I don't need any more curves than I already have. But I can't resist a good cookie."

She snatches a cookie from the display case. "This is a Blackbeard's revenge cookie. You'll love it."

"Blackbeard's revenge?"

"Everything on the island is mermaid or smuggler themed."

I snort. "I know all about the mermaids."

"Don't worry. The mermaids only last for about six weeks of the summer during Mermaid Karaoke season."

"Mermaid Karaoke season?"

"Yep. You should avoid the *Bootlegger* bar until the summer's over."

In my dreams I have time to barhop. "*Bootlegger?* You weren't kidding about the smuggler theme."

"Nope." She sets a plate with the cookie on the counter. "What kind of coffee do you want?"

"Anything with caffeine is my favorite."

"Double espresso coming up." She shoos me toward a table. "Go. Sit down. I'll bring your coffee over."

I settle at a spot in front of the window. I nibble on my cookie as I watch people pass by. I realize I'm tasting air and glance down at my shirt where half of my cookie has landed.

Parker hands me a napkin. "It happens to the best of us."

"Except it happens to me all the time," I mutter as I wipe away the crumbs. All I succeed in doing is creating a giant chocolate stain.

"What happened to you?" a woman asks as she sits across from me.

"A cookie attacked me."

"Gotta hate when that happens." She sips on my coffee and moans. "Mmm... Parker I'll have one of these."

I glide the mug across the table toward her. "You can have mine."

"I'll make you another one," Parker says before walking away.

"Thanks." The woman salutes me with the mug. "I needed this."

Probably not as much as I did, I start to say, but stop myself. There's no reason to be snarky to this stranger. I don't know her. Maybe she does need the caffeine as much as I do.

"Why are you desperate for a caffeine hit?" I ask.

"My boss had me up most of the night."

"Who's your boss? Hold on. Who are you?"

"I'm Blossom. I was the newcomer before you."

"I'm Dakota," I say despite having a sneaking suspicion she already knows my name. "Does everyone know everyone's business here?"

She shrugs. "Pretty much. You get used to it. Personally, I prefer it over going to the grocery store and not seeing one friendly face."

"I know how you feel," I mutter. Grocery shopping is not fun when everyone in the cereal aisle is glaring at you, or the women waiting to check out switch lanes to avoid you. It does make doing groceries much quicker, though.

"Here's your coffee," Parker says as she sets a steaming mug in front of me.

"Thank…" I trail off when I notice a furry head pop up from her pocket. "Do you have a puppy in your pocket?"

"You were supposed to stay hidden," she tells the animal as she removes it from her pocket and cuddles it.

"That's not a dog," Blossom says.

"She's an otter. Her name is Viking."

"You named your girl otter Viking?" I ask.

"Technically, she's not mine."

"Are you otter-sitting? Is otter-sitting a thing? Where do I sign up?" I ask as I reach a hand out to pet Viking.

The little creature leans into my palm. "She's adorable. Why isn't she yours?"

"She's the town mascot."

"The town has a mascot? What does a live mascot do for a town? It can't exactly throw the first pitch at a baseball game."

Blossom giggles. "The mascots are strictly forbidden from attending sports events."

"You're serious?"

"I blame my boss."

This is the second time she's mentioned her boss. I'm officially intrigued. "Who's your boss?"

"Paisley. She's part-owner of the brewery in town, *Five Fathoms.*"

"And it's her fault mascots are forbidden from attending sports events? I'm confused."

Parker giggles. "Welcome to Smuggler's Hideaway. Each town on the island has a mascot. Smuggler's Rest has Viking here. Rogue's Landing has Rogue, the raccoon. And Pirate's Perch has Plank, the parrot. Each summer the inhabitants of the towns try to steal the mascot of another town."

"Why? And how? Raccoons are mean."

"It's a long-standing tradition. Whoever manages to steal the mascot from another town has eternal bragging rights." Parker rubs her nose against Viking's. "But no one's going to steal you, are they?"

"Shouldn't you keep the location of the otter a secret if you don't want anyone to steal it?"

She taps his nose. "Viking being here is supposed to be a secret, but the little rascal keeps stealing my cookies."

"Don't you have a cage for her?"

Parker's lips purse. "Nobody puts Viking in the corner."

I giggle. "I don't think the saying refers to an otter who steals cookies."

Blossom holds out her hands. "Can I hold her? She's so cute."

Parker places Viking in Blossom's hands. But the little rascal doesn't stay there. She jumps onto the table and goes for my plate. When she notices the plate is empty, she sniffs the air and her gaze lands on my t-shirt.

I lean away from the table but I'm not quick enough. Viking launches herself onto my lap before crawling under my shirt. She scurries up my shirt and peeks her head out of my collar.

I pet her. "You're a troublemaker." I kiss her nose. "The cutest troublemaker in the world."

Parker moans. "Now, she's going to think it's okay to jump under people's shirts."

I hand her the otter. "Maybe you should reconsider the cage thing."

A buzzer goes off in the kitchen. "Be right back."

Once she's out of hearing range, Blossom leans close and whispers, "I think we should steal Viking."

"Steal Viking?"

"You heard Parker, we'd have bragging rights forever. I bet we'd get free drinks at *Rumrunner*."

"What's *Rumrunner?*"

"It's a speakeasy. We'll go there for our first girls' night out."

My eyes widen. "Our first girls' night out?"

"Yep." She grins. "I've decided we're going to be best friends."

"What if I already have a best friend?"

My best friend couldn't dump me fast enough when she found out my husband had a thing for hookers and gambling, but I'm not telling Blossom my sad story. Sad stories are meant for late nights when you've had too many cosmos and forget to keep your mouth shut. Not for sunny days sitting at a pirate-themed bakery eating yummy treats and petting a cute otter.

"We'll add her name to the guest list at *Rumrunner*."

"Guest list?"

"*Rumrunner* is a speakeasy. If you're not on the guest list, you have to solve a riddle." Her nose wrinkles. "I hate riddles."

"I rather enjoy riddles."

"Fine. You can answer the riddle. I'll be inside on my second glass of moonshine by the time you figure it out."

"Moonshine?"

"The island's famous for it."

My brow wrinkles. "Is there anything this island isn't famous for?"

She bursts into laughter. "You're getting it."

Warmth fills me. I didn't understand half of what she said and I'm confused about the speakeasy and live mascots, but I don't care. I made a friend today.

I only hope she'll remain my friend when she figures out I don't have money to spend on a girls' night out.

Chapter 6

"Pranks are forbidden in the office from now on." ~
Rhett

RHETT

"Dakota," I grumble in greeting as I pass her desk.

She smiles at me and her green eyes sparkle. "Good morning."

I narrow my eyes on her. Why is she being pleasant? Is she up to something?

She blinks up at me. "Can I help you? Technically, I'm Eli's employee and not an employee of the distillery, but I can try to help."

Ah, now I understand. She thinks she's won. She has no idea who she's dealing with.

I grunt before continuing to my office.

"A grunt is not an answer," she hollers after me. I shut my door in response.

I don't have time to unravel the mystery of Dakota this morning. I need to finish the quarterly reports. I roll up my sleeves and get to work.

"What the hell?" I mutter to my computer. I backspace and retype the word 'report' but the second I finish typing the word 'report' becomes 'banana'.

In Q2, Buccaneer's Whiskey & Distillery demonstrated strong financial performance with notable increases in revenue, gross profit, and net profit. This banana provides an in-depth analysis of key financial metrics, expense categories, and sales performance.

"This banana? It's supposed to be report. What is wrong with my computer? KAI!"

If my brother pranked me again, I'm going to throw him into a vat of whiskey and Jaxon won't be able to stop me.

"What's up, buttercup?" Kai asks as he strolls into my office.

I point to my computer. "What did you do?"

He rolls back on his heels. "What do you think I did?"

"Answer the question," I demand.

"I can't answer the question if I don't know what you're talking about."

I jump to my feet. "You know what you did. Now, fix it before I bash your head in with my monitor."

He tsks. "Now. Now. Now. You shouldn't threaten violence at the office. I believe human resources would frown upon any and all violent actions."

"Good thing I'm in charge of human resources and decide what's violent or not."

He sighs. "How sad. You're abusing your power again."

"I am not abusing my power. Now, fix my computer. Unlike you, I have work to do."

His brow wrinkles. "And I don't?"

"You wouldn't know what being on time was if it hit you on the ass."

"What does my refusal to accept the construct of time have to do with anything?"

I thread my hands through my hair and pull on the ends before I fly at my brother. Mom will tan my hide if I hurt her precious baby. Precious baby, my ass.

"Time is not a construct devised by modern society to put the man down," I grit out.

Kai crosses his arms over his chest. "Why are there clocks everywhere if society isn't trying to shape me into a time following sheep?"

I've had it. I don't care what Mom does. I'm throwing Kai out the window. We're on the first floor. He'll survive. He'll have a few bruises but bruises are character building.

Zane strolls into my office. "What's going on?"

Kai points to me. "The old man is having a hissy fit."

"I'm a grown man. I don't have hissy fits."

Zane studies me. "Your face is turning red, your eyes are bulging, and a vein in your neck is pulsing. I believe this is the classic definition of a hissy fit."

I slam my fist down on the table. "I am not having a hissy fit."

Zane and Kai look at each other. "Hissy fit," they say in unison.

"Fix my computer!"

Kai holds up his hands. "I'm not a computer guru."

I point at my desk. "But you fucked up my computer."

He shrugs. "I can ask Jaxon to have a look. He can probably read a manual about computers and be able to program a rocket launch within a few hours."

"But would he want to?" Zane asks. "He is pretty obsessed with the mixology of whisky."

"I'm not complaining. Our whiskey is the best."

I scowl. Why are they speaking about whiskey and not fixing my computer?

"Will you please stop speaking in circles and fix my computer?"

Zane steps closer to my desk. "What's wrong with it? Nothing seems out of sorts."

"Someone," I growl, "messed with the autocorrect."

"Really?" Kai raises an eyebrow. "What does the autocorrect do?"

"You know this. Whenever I type 'report', it switches the word to 'banana'."

Kai barks out a laugh. "Brilliant."

"Oh man." Zane grins. "I wish I could take credit."

"Miles!" I shout.

Dakota sweeps into my office. "Miles isn't here. He left a message about the waves calling his name."

I snatch my keys from my desk. "I'll show him what calling his name means."

I march toward the door.

"I'm wondering," Dakota begins, and I pause.

"Wondering what?"

"If you assume one of your brothers pranked you because they prank you all the time? Or are you one of those men who thinks women are stupid?"

I frown. "Women aren't stupid."

She crosses her arms over her chest. "And yet you don't think a woman could have messed with your autocorrect."

"I never said ..." I trail off when I realize what she means. "You?" She nods. "You messed with my computer?"

Her nose wrinkles. "I wouldn't say messed."

"Messed sounds sexual," Kai says.

Her lips purse. "Sexual?"

I nearly groan at the word sexual coming out of those pretty bowtie lips Dakota has. Those lips I've imagined touching with my own way too often. I wonder how she tastes. I bet whatever it is, is addictive.

"There's nothing sexual about putting Mr. High and Mighty in his place."

Any thoughts of tasting her fly out the window at her words. "You did this?"

She bats her eyelashes. "It wasn't hard."

My cock twitches. It enjoys the word 'hard' emitting from her lips. It wants to show her how hard it can be.

My nostrils flare. "You fucked with my computer and wasted my time."

She fists her hands on her hips. "Maybe this will teach you I'm not an idiot you can have fired because you don't approve of the car I drive."

"I didn't say a word about your car."

"It was implied, bossypants."

Kai chuckles. "Bossypants. The name fits."

I glare at him and Zane. "The two of you out of here now!"

"Sorry, bossypants. No can do." Zane waves a hand at my face. "You look as if you're about to have a stroke. I can't leave this sweet, innocent woman alone with you."

Sweet and innocent? Dakota is devious, and she's obviously keeping secrets from us. I will not allow some woman to come in here and ruin the business we've built as a family. No one will destroy this family. Not even our father.

"Promise to stop going behind my back to try and get me fired and I'll fix your computer," Dakota offers.

"You should fix my computer because I told you so."

She shrugs. "No skin off my back," she says as she strolls for the door.

"Stop!" I order.

She glances over her shoulder at me. "I don't take orders from men who are trying to control me."

"I love you!" Zane shouts.

"I love you, too," Kai agrees. "Everyone thinks we're exaggerating when we complain about how controlling Rhett is."

"For the last time, it's not controlling when I order you to make your bed."

Zane's nose wrinkles. "I don't understand what the big deal is. You just sleep in the bed again at night and it gets all wrinkled again. What's the point?"

"Everyone, stop distracting me. Dakota, fix my computer now before I tell Eli."

"Tell me what?" Eli asks as he pokes his head into the room.

"She," I stab my finger toward Dakota, "messed with my autocorrect."

"And I told him I'd fix it if he'd stop going behind my back to try and get me fired."

Eli grins at her. "You're going to fit in here just fine."

"What the hell? You're not going to yell at her for messing with my computer?"

Eli frowns at me. "You tried to get her fired. Did you think she'd accept your actions lying down?"

"Whatever." I motion to my desk. "Fix my computer."

She crosses her arms over her chest. "Promise you won't try to get me fired again."

"I promise I won't get you fired," I grit out.

I do reserve the right to voice my concerns over her work with Eli. I will never allow anyone to abuse this family. It's my job to protect my brothers no matter how much they annoy the shit out of me.

And the first task in my protection duties is to figure out what secrets Dakota is keeping.

Chapter 7

DAKOTA

"Did you finish the list?" Eli asks.

I hold up my clipboard. "All done."

"Good." He squeezes my shoulder. "Get home and get safe. A hurricane of this size can cause a lot of damage."

"But a house is safe?"

I didn't think about the possibility of hurricanes when I moved to an island on the Atlantic coast. But now I'm wishing I had. Because the sound of the wind is freaking me out and the hurricane isn't even here yet. It isn't expected to hit land for several hours.

"Of course, it is. All homes on Smuggler's Hideaway constructed after 1970 have been built to withstand hurricanes."

1970? The *Mermaid Motel* is from the 1950s. Is it not safe?

Sadie evacuated all the guests, but she assured me I'd be perfectly safe in my suite. If the guests weren't safe, why am I? She had no answer to my question.

I force a smile. "Great. I'll grab my purse and lock up. You go ahead."

"Thanks for all your help, Dakota. We couldn't have done it without you."

I smirk. "You'd be lost without me."

"Take care," he says before leaving.

I grab my purse and keys. My heart thumps in my chest. I don't want to abandon the protection of this sturdy building to stay in a motel with the thinnest walls in existence, but what choice do I have?

None. I open the door to leave. The wind smacks me in the face and the door smashes into the side of the building. Damn. This is worse than I thought.

Rhett argued we should board up the door for protection, but Eli insisted the building is hurricane proof and the door didn't need to be protected.

Hurricane proof? The reminder is all I need to know. I fight the door but eventually I win. When the door is finally shut, I'm not outside in the parking lot. I'm inside. Where I hope I'll be safe.

According to Google, I should take refuge in a small interior room on the lowest level. I need to put as many walls between me and the outside as I can.

The closet in Eli's office should be perfect. I gather bottles of water and protein bars from the breakroom, a blanket from the sofa in Miles's office, and a flashlight from my desk before making my way to Eli's office.

I carefully lay Eli's coats and extra suits on one of the chairs in his office before making myself a blanket fort and settling in to ride out the storm.

"What are you doing in here?"

I startle awake at the question and open my eyes. A light shines into them and I slam them shut again. "What? Who?"

"Dakota," Rhett murmurs, and I force my eyes open. His flashlight is no longer pointed at my face. He kneels in front of me. "What are you doing in here?"

"Is it over?"

"The storm?"

"It was so windy and loud."

He sighs. "No, it's not over."

"What are you doing here if there's a hurricane out there?"

"The police phoned about an abandoned car in the parking lot."

"Do not make fun of my car."

He holds up his hands. "I wasn't going to." He smirks. "But it wouldn't be surprising if the ancient relic died in the parking lot."

I gasp. "Don't say such a thing. Matilda isn't ancient."

He chuckles. "Matilda? You named your car?"

"Matilda means brave."

And since I wasn't feeling very brave when I bought the car, I forced myself to be brave by naming her Matilda. Fake it until you make it.

"No matter how brave Matilda is, she's not going anywhere now."

"I wasn't planning on going outside in a hurricane anyway." No thanks. I'm good in my blanket fort. The winds before the storm landed were scary enough.

He nudges my shoulder. "Scoot over."

"Why? I'm comfy here."

"It's safer if we shut the closet door."

"We? What are you talking about?"

"I can hardly go back out in the storm."

"But you came out in the storm."

He glances away. "Because I was worried about you."

I blink. "You were worried about me? The man who has the victory party planned for when I'm fired?"

"I wouldn't say planned. Does renting a venue count?"

I giggle. "I hope you didn't put down a deposit because I am not getting fired."

He shrugs. "They said the deposit is refundable."

I feign surprise and let my jaw drop open. "Rhett Raider, did you make a joke?"

"I can joke."

"Really? Your brothers are convinced you're a robot."

"My brothers are assholes."

I elbow him. "Don't speak about your family that way. Families are special."

At least, I assume they are. I've never had one. Don't mistake me. Growing up in care wasn't horrific. At least, not for me it wasn't. Did I have warm and fuzzy foster parents? I did not. But they were decent people who fed and clothed me and made sure I got my homework done. They also had more foster kids than they knew what to do with. They didn't have time for hugs or cuddles.

Rhett sighs before using his hip to nudge me further into the closet. The touch of his body has mine feeling all warm and fuzzy. I ignore it. I'm obviously a bad judge of men. A former husband who gambled our money away and a man who wants to fire me. Totally bad judge of men.

Once Rhett's inside, he shuts the door behind him and sets a lantern on the floor to illuminate the area.

"Do you have any food? I'm starved."

I gather my bag of food and hug it close to me. "No way. You'll finish up my supplies in five minutes, and who knows how long the storm will last."

"Are you saying I'm a pig?"

"No, I'm saying your muscles have muscles and they need fuel."

And I'm not saying I want to touch those muscles. Or trace them with my tongue. Nope. Not I. See the aforementioned remark regarding my abysmal taste in men.

He flexes his bicep. "Are you impressed?"

"I'm more impressed with brains than with brawn."

He waggles his eyebrows. "What if I have both?"

"Then, you wouldn't have written a report about bananas even though you're the CFO of a distillery."

"Because someone messed with my computer."

I roll my eyes. "If you had brains, you'd know how to fix it. It's really simple."

"Really simple?"

"Yep." I nod. "Super simple. A baby could do it."

"Could a baby do this?"

He tickles my ribs and I giggle. I've always been super ticklish.

"Stop it." I bat at his hands. "No tickling. I'll pee myself."

He freezes. "You can't pee yourself when we're stuck in a closet together."

"Good thing I have the strongest bladder of anyone I know."

He narrows his eyes on me. "You said you'd pee if I tickled you."

"Got you to stop, didn't I?"

"But now I know you're ticklish."

"And I know you're afraid of the smell of pee."

He grunts. "If you had my five brothers, you'd be afraid of the smell of urine, too. Putting your hand in warm water while you're sleeping won't make you pee. But tricking your brother into drinking a gallon of water before bed and then daring him not to use the bathroom all night will."

My nose wrinkles. "Ew. Who wet the bed?"

"Kai but you can never let him know I told. We had to do a blood oath of secrecy."

"Why would you do a blood oath of secrecy? This is prime teasing material."

"Kai made us swear to secrecy or he was going to tell Mom about the time we broke her oven."

"How did you break an oven? I've had plenty of cooking mishaps, and I've never broken an oven. A microwave, maybe, but never an oven."

"Remind me to remove the microwave from the break room."

I slap him. "I broke the microwave when I was ten. No one told me you can't put aluminum foil in a microwave."

He rolls his eyes. "Because it's common knowledge."

"Not in the foster home I lived in."

He leans closer. "You grew up in care?"

Crap. I don't want to talk about my past. My past leads from foster care to jumping into bed with the first man who pretended to care for me, to marrying him, to becoming a widow in dire need of money. No one wants to hear my pathetic story. Least of all me.

"Rhett!" Eli shouts. "Dakota! Where are you?"

Rhett kneels to open the closet door. "We're in here."

Eli stares down at us. "Why are you hiding in a closet?"

"It's supposed to be the safest place during a hurricane," I say.

"Lucky for you. The hurricane is over."

"Awesome. I'm out of here." I climb over Rhett and Eli offers his hand to help me up.

I stretch my muscles and twist my neck to relieve the stiffness from being cramped in a closet with Rhett for who knows how long.

Rhett, who laughed and joked with me. Rhett, who told me secrets about my family. Rhett, whose body was a source of heat.

No. No. No. Stop it, Dakota. You are not developing a crush on the man who's trying to fire you.

But maybe he won't try to fire me anymore? I glance up at him from beneath my lashes. Maybe this is the start of a friendship.

The lights flicker on and I blink my eyes at the assault of light. I notice the clock on the wall and swear.

"Oh crap. Is that the time? I need to…"

I rush off without finishing my sentence. My truce with Rhett is a fragile thing. If he figures out I'm sick, he might go back to trying to get me fired. And I need the health insurance. More than I need a friend.

Chapter 8

"Go ahead. Steal my shoe. See what happens." ~
Rhett

RHETT

"Did you bring your lucky charm?" Kai asks.

I grunt.

Miles wags his finger at me. "Grunting isn't an answer, Mr. High and Mighty."

"I am not Mr. High and Mighty," I grumble.

"Oh, sorry. I didn't realize your girlfriend, Dakota, is the only one who can use the nickname."

"Not my girlfriend."

"I heard they were cozied up in Eli's closet during the hurricane," Zane says.

"I heard Eli caught them naked in his shower," Kai claims.

"We were not naked in Eli's shower," I grumble.

I've never been naked with Dakota. The only time I touched her was to tickle her. I barely touched her ribs and my cock was ready to explode out of my pants.

But I won't be touching her again. Not after how she ran off when Eli arrived. It's obvious she's keeping secrets. But what are they? And will they ruin the company? My family? My idiot brothers already love her, but I won't allow anyone else to break their hearts. Not after what Dad did. Never again.

"Are we going to play poker? Or are we going to tease Rhett about Dakota all night long?" Jaxon asks.

Miles throws his arm over Jaxon's shoulders. "Don't you worry. We're also going to tease Eli about Paisley all night long."

Eli's had a crush on Paisley since high school. When the hurricane ruined her brewing facilities – she's part owner of the *Five Fathoms* brewery here on the island – he couldn't rush to her side quick enough to offer her use of the extra space in the distillery.

We were planning to use the space to expand the distillery but the hurricane and the local brewery needing help put those plans on hold. I don't mind. I'm happy Eli is occupied with Paisley instead of working himself to death.

Eli clears his throat. "It's my house. Tease me and I'm kicking you out."

Zane bursts into laughter. "As if you can keep us out."

Eli glares at him. "You are not crawling in through the window in my fitness room again."

Zane shivers. "No way. The window is tiny."

Kai wiggles a set of keys in the air. "Good thing we have the keys."

"And the alarm code," Miles adds.

Eli rubs a hand down his face. "How the hell did you get my alarm codes?"

"Ask me no questions and I'll tell you no lies," Miles sings.

"Hey! Where are you going?" Zane points at Jaxon, who's opening the front door. "Let me guess, our nerdy brother has too much work to do to spend time with his family."

Jaxon removes his glasses and pinches his nose. "I'm required to attend poker night, but if we're not playing poker, I have work to do."

Eli frowns. "Do I need to hire you an assistant?"

Jaxon scowls. "I don't need an assistant."

"If you need to work on a Friday night after you've already worked fifty hours this week, you need an assistant. I'll set up a meeting with you and Dakota on Monday. You can go through your requirements for an assistant."

"I don't need Dakota's help," Jaxon insists.

"But Rhett does." Kai waggles his eyebrows.

I start toward him. I'm done with my brothers and their teasing about Dakota. Do I want Dakota in my bed? Hell yeah, I do. The woman is sexy as hell with those bowtie lips, green eyes, and curves for days.

But I don't fool around with women who are obviously liars. I thought we might have something. When we were stuck in the closet during the hurricane, we laughed and joked, and she opened up to me about growing up in care.

Except it was all a mirage. The second the hurricane was over, she ran away. She was being all sneaky. What is she up to? What are her secrets? I will find out.

Eli steps in front of me. "No fighting. You're the one who's supposed to keep these yahoos under control, remember?"

I remember. How could I forget? It's been my full-time job since Dad up and left us when I was fifteen.

"I'm with Jaxon. If we're not playing poker, I'm out of here."

"But Nugget wants to play poker." Zane holds up his taxidermized squirrel. It's wearing a cowboy hat because, of course, it is. This is Zane after all.

"Nugget's getting his ass kicked by Mr. Crisp." Kai cuddles a jar containing a pickle he's named Mr. Crisp. The pickle is apparently wise and full of poker wisdom.

Miles dangles his rabbit's foot. "Hopper is feeling lucky tonight."

Zane points to the foot. "Hopper is not a bunny. No rabbit has ever had a foot that big or lumpy."

"Says the man holding a squirrel in a cowboy hat."

Zane hugs the squirrel. "Do not make fun of Nugget. He's a gentle soul."

Eli sighs. "Whose idea was it to play poker with lucky items?"

Miles wags his finger at him. "Says the man whose lucky item is a pair of teeth."

"Because those teeth scared the hell out of you when you were younger. It was the only way I could get you to brush your teeth."

Eli used to chase Miles – and Kai and Zane – around the house while snapping the teeth at them. More than one pair of pants was peed in fright.

Zane elbows Miles. "Better a set of teeth than a lonely bowling shoe."

"Leave me out of this," I insist.

"One shoe is kind of lame," Miles adds.

"I'll have you know I won the bowling championship in junior year while wearing this one shoe because you shits stole my other shoe."

Kai widens his eyes. "I have no idea what you're referring to. I would never steal someone's shoe."

I cross my arms and glare at him. "Which is why I found it under your bed."

He throws his hands in the air. "I was framed. I didn't put it there."

"Where did you put it?"

"I mean. I didn't have the shoe at all. I didn't take it."

He's lying. I caught the little thief running away with my shoe. But I didn't have time to chase him because I was already late for the bowling championships. I thought I could rent another shoe at the bowling alley. But they were out of rentals. I still won despite wearing a sock on one foot.

Eli claps me on the back. "You are never going to win this argument."

Don't I know it. "Let's play some poker."

We follow Eli down the hallway to his game room. I don't envy my oldest brother his wealth. He can have the fancy mansion with the indoor pool and eleven guest rooms. But this room? This room I'd fight my brothers for.

The walls are paneled and painted a deep green color. Along one wall is a bar and – because this is my billionaire brother – it's stocked with every high-end whiskey you can imagine, including our own *Buccaneer's Whiskey*. The opposite side of the room has two leather couches. Naturally, there's a large television to watch the game on. In the middle of the room are the games – a poker table big enough to seat six and a pool table.

Eli aims for the bar. "What does everyone want to drink? *Blackbeard's Reserve?*"

"I want *Siren's Call*," Zane says.

Jaxon purses his lips. "Do not drink too much. It's stronger than rum."

Zane moans. "Will everyone stop referring to the time I drank too much rum? Every one of you has had too much to drink at one time or another."

Miles snorts. "But we didn't make the entire house smell of coconuts after we threw up Malibu Rum for two days straight."

"*Cursed Treasure* it is." Eli sets a bottle of whiskey down on the poker table.

"A whiskey so good, it might have a ghostly secret. Not a bad slogan if I do say so myself." Zane feigns polishing his fingers on his shirt.

Miles rolls his eyes. "Yea. Yea. Yea. You're the marketing genius behind the brand."

"It's good you recognize I'm a genius."

Miles raises his hand but I shackle his wrist. "No hitting at the poker table."

"You're boring." Miles yanks his hand away and reaches for a glass of whiskey.

Eli holds his glass up. "Here's to the bootleggers. Masters of sneaky sips and secret stashes."

"Thanks for keeping the party alive," we finish the Smuggler's Hideaway toast in unison.

I barely stop myself from grimacing as fire burns through my esophagus. Despite owning a distillery, I'm not much of a drinker.

Jaxon sets his Chia Pet on the table. "If we're ready to begin."

"It's not time for your 'Elvis' to lose quite yet," Kai says.

"What's with the air quotes? My Chia Pet clearly resembles Elvis. I won the contest."

Miles chuckles. "Did anyone else enter the contest?"

"What is the losing prize for today?" Eli asks before Jaxon and Miles can get into another argument about the Chia Pet. It's a monthly recurrence. And one all of us are sick to death of listening to.

"I have t-shirts picked out for the loser," Kai says.

"Don't you mean t-shirt?" I ask. "There can only be one loser."

Kai smirks. "But each t-shirt is different depending on who the loser is." He points to me. "For Mr. High and Mighty, I have a t-shirt which says 'Dakota, will you marry me?'"

I growl. I will not be marrying the secret keeper. No matter how much my cock perks up at the idea of having access to her every day. It's not happening.

"For Eli, the t-shirt says, 'I'm wealthy and I know it.'"

Eli scowls. "I will never wear a t-shirt proclaiming I'm wealthy."

Kai rubs his hands together. "You will if you lose at poker."

I grab the deck and remove the packaging. We use a new deck every month as these pranksters can't be trusted not to mark up the cards. They're cheaters down to their toes.

Out of the corner of my eye, I notice Zane reaching for my shoe. I slap his hand. "Don't touch my shoe."

"But if I steal your shoe, you lose and have to wear the t-shirt."

"I am not wearing a fucking t-shirt asking Dakota to marry me."

Even if I were interested in a relationship – which I'm not – it wouldn't be with Dakota. But I will uncover what secrets she's hiding. And, after I do, Eli will rush to fire her.

And then she'll be out of our lives forever. I ignore how my stomach sours. This is the way it has to be.

Chapter 9

DAKOTA

The door opens, and I smile at Rhett. "Good morning."

He grunts in response.

"There's coffee in the breakroom for those of us who aren't morning people."

He doesn't even bother to grunt this time. He passes my desk without glancing my way. Someone is not a morning person. I don't love mornings either but I haven't gone to bed yet since my shift at the motel is from midnight to six a.m.

I stopped by Pirates Pastries for coffee and a snuggle with Viking this morning before coming to work. The caffeine hit should last me for at least an hour.

I hope. My sleeping schedule is completely out a whack. I try to sleep for five hours after I get home from the distillery. Then, I work eight hours behind the desk where I cat nap from four until six.

On Saturday, I sleep all day and on Sunday, I catch up on all my housework. It's a brutal schedule. I don't know how long I can keep this up.

I force my attention back to work. It's my job to read all of Eli's emails. He gets a ton of emails from people begging for money or mentorship or a job or an investment or …The list goes on and on. It's crazy. I can barely keep up.

An hour later, I finish with the emails and make my way to the break room. It's the prettiest breakroom I've ever seen – there are actual Baccarat crystal glasses – although I don't have much to compare it with. I worked for a plumbing company before this. I was glad if the counter and coffee machine there weren't tainted with dirty handprints.

Rhett is in the room when I arrive.

"Hey, blanket fort buddy. How are you?"

He scowls at me. "Blanket fort buddy?"

"Did you forget we spent a hurricane bundled under a blanket in a closet together?"

I'm never going to forget. Before Rhett arrived, I was terrified. After he joined me, I didn't feel scared at all. Maybe a bit scared of how my body yearns for the controlling man. But it's a good kind of scared. An exciting kind.

I've spent more time than I care to admit daydreaming about how he touched me when we were in the closet. What would have happened if I hadn't told him tickling makes me pee? Would he have glided his hands to my breasts? My nipples tingle at the idea. Or maybe south? My panties dampen.

"I wasn't under a blanket."

"I forgot. Your body radiates enough heat to warm Antarctica in the middle of the coldest winter night."

He frowns.

"Do you still refer to it as night when it's dark twenty-four hours a day?"

"Stop."

My brow wrinkles. "Stop what? Are you an Antarctica hater? Oh no. Are you one of those conspiracy theorists who believe the world is flat and therefore Antarctica doesn't exist? What does Eli think of you being a conspiracy theorist? I'm surprised he hasn't bundled you off to some rehabilitation center to disabuse you of your ideas."

"I don't hate Antarctica."

"Phew." I run the back of my hand over my brow. "I was worried there for a second. It wouldn't have stopped me from spending all my time putting articles about how flat-earthers are wrong everywhere in your office, though. Conspiracy theories are scary and should be stopped."

"You should be stopped."

I hold up a hand. "I'm not going to plant articles about flat earthers everywhere. I said I *would have,* not I *will.*"

"I meant stop talking."

"Are you telling me to shut up? Have you not had enough coffee yet?"

He sighs. "I think you're confused."

"I'm not confused. You've made yourself clear. You understand the Earth is round. Noted."

He growls. "I'm not discussing the Earth. I mean about us."

"What do you mean? Us? What us?"

"Exactly." He nods. "There is no us."

"I didn't say there was. Hold on. Did you think I think we're a couple because we spent a day in a closet together? Weirdest first date ever."

"It wasn't a date."

"I know. I said the same thing two seconds ago."

"You're speaking in circles."

"I never understood that phrase. Am I walking in circles while I'm speaking? Are my sentences circular? Admit it. It's a weird phrase."

He holds up a hand. "Please stop. You're giving me a headache."

"I'm giving you a headache? If we weren't friends, I'd be offended."

"That's the point. We aren't friends."

My stomach dives to the floor at his words. "We're not? But I thought…"

I trail off because it doesn't matter what I thought. Once again, I was wrong about a man. At least I didn't jump into bed with this one before realizing what an asshole he is.

He doesn't respond. He merely stares at me as if I'm a fool. Message received.

"Okay." I nod. "You've made yourself clear. We're not friends."

I whirl around and stomp out of the breakroom.

What an asshole! I thought Rhett just had a hard time warming up to people. Which I could understand since he lives on a small island and I'm an outsider.

But he's not having a hard time warming up to me. He's just a plain old jerkity jerk.

If he thinks he can get away with being nice to me before dropping a 'we're not friends'-bomb, he's wrong. Considering how the auto-correct prank drove him nuts, I believe another prank is in order.

I wake my computer to research ideas.

An hour later, I hear Rhett's door open. He makes his way to the breakroom. I wait until he's inside before following him.

He glances over his shoulder at me. He scowls before lifting the coffee pot. I shake my head. I am not drinking that coffee. I nearly giggle but I clear my throat before any laughter escapes. I don't want him to be suspicious.

He probably thinks I followed him in here like a lost puppy after he kicked me. I'm no lost puppy and I have some pride. Not much after the whole fiasco with Adam. But I'm building it up again.

Rhett doesn't want to be friends. We're not friends. I will not beg him for attention.

I open the refrigerator and take out a bottle of water for a reason to be here. I twist open the top and sip on the water as I wait for him to taste his coffee.

He brings the cup to his mouth and I hide my face behind the water bottle before my excitement gives me away. He sips and his brow wrinkles. He takes another sip before gagging and spitting the coffee out in the sink.

"What the hell?"

I flutter my eyelashes. "What the hell what? What's wrong?" I lay the innocence on thick.

"The coffee's gone bad."

"Gone bad? Can coffee go bad? I didn't realize."

He narrows his eyes on me. "What did you do to the coffee?"

"What? What do you mean?"

He nods to my water. "You never drink water in the morning. You mainline coffee all morning. In the afternoon, you intermix your coffee drinking with water."

Someone's been paying attention. Don't go feeling flattered, Dakota. This man is not interested in me.

"Thanks for paying attention, bossypants." I wink.

He growls. "What the hell did you do to the coffee?"

"I didn't do anything to the coffee."

Lies. All lies.

"It tastes like shit."

"And you have experience with tasting shit?"

"Stop being cute."

My stomach flutters. Knock it off. Not interested in me, remember?

Zane and Miles stroll into the room. "What's going on? Are we having a meeting?" Zane asks.

Miles scowls. "No, thanks."

"No meeting", Rhett grumbles. "Someone messed with the coffee."

"It wasn't me," Miles and Zane answer in unison.

Rhett points to me. "A female someone."

Miles meets my gaze. "I'm loving you more and more."

Zane shoves him. "I loved her first."

"Shut up!" Rhett yells. "She fucked with the coffee."

"High five." Miles lifts his palm and – what the hell – I high-five him.

"You did mess with the coffee. I fucking knew it."

"My. My. Someone's language is atrocious today," Zane says. "If I spoke those words, you'd threaten to wash my mouth out with soap."

"Stop distracting me." Rhett waves the coffee pot my way. "Who do you think you are? Coming in to this company, screwing things up, and dividing us brothers."

"Whoa, dude." Miles steps in front of me. "You're out of line."

I peek out from behind him. "I haven't screwed anything up and I'm not pitting the brothers against you."

From what I can tell, Miles and Zane drive Rhett crazy all on their own. No help from little old me needed. Although, I am always willing to lend a hand. I'm helpful that way.

Rhett raises the coffee pot before throwing it across the room. It slams into the wall and smashes into a million pieces while coffee flies in the air.

My mouth drops open. "What is wrong with you? It was a little prank. And you know exactly why I pranked you." I pause but he doesn't deign to apologize for his behavior. "Dickhead.

I'll have maintenance come clean this up and order a new coffee pot."

I hurry out of the room and make my way to the restroom. I lock the door behind me before leaning against it. My heart pounds in my chest.

Rhett's anger was out of proportion to what happened. And I'm not afraid to admit it scared me a little bit.

Another sign I don't know how to pick men. The universe keeps dropping them in front of me.

I hear you, universe. I got it. Rhett is not the man for me. No more signs necessary.

Chapter 10

"My jaw is innocent." ~ Rhett

RHETT

I set the plant on Dakota's desk. She doesn't bother to deign to lift her head to meet my gaze. I can't blame her.

I was a total asshole. First, I claim we're not friends. Then, I overreact to her prank and throw a coffee pot.

I wait for her to respond to me but she continues to type away on her keyboard as if I don't exist. Harsh.

"This is for you."

"Thanks," she mutters.

"I'm sorry."

She sighs before finally glancing my way. "Sorry for what? Being cruel or being violent?"

My feisty girl is back. I nearly smile. "Both?"

"Are you asking or saying?"

"Saying. Both. Sorry for being a dick."

"Don't do it again. I suck at avoiding you. The hallway closet is small and smelly. I don't want to spend any more time in there."

I chuckle. "There's no reason to avoid me. I promise not to throw any more coffee pots around."

"Good. Because Eli lost his mind. The coffee machine is some fancy brand exclusive for billionaires and it'll be another week before the replacement pot is here. He is one unhappy puppy."

Damn. I guess I better buy another plant for Eli.

"Rhett!" Eli shouts.

"His majesty awaits. Don't make the bossman wait."

I rap my knuckles on her desk before walking down the hallway to Eli's office.

"What's up?" I ask as I settle into a chair across from his desk.

"We voted to expand the distillery last month, but the expansion is on hold."

I nod. "I'm aware."

It's impossible to miss since the local brewery, *Five Fathoms Brewing,* moved their brewing facilities into the extra space in the distillery. *Five Fathoms* was destroyed by the hurricane and Eli stepped in to help them. Although, his charitable efforts were more to help Paisley, the head brewer he's obsessed with.

"Before the hurricane, I closed an exclusive deal to supply the Velvet Blossom restaurant chain with our whiskeys. Technically, we could claim force majeure and get out of the deal."

I can read between the lines. "But you don't want to."

"The brewery won't be here forever." He doesn't appear happy about the idea. Probably because Paisley and him get up to all kinds of sexy shenanigans when they should be working. They think no one knows. Everyone knows.

"What do you want from me?"

"I have a meeting scheduled with the board of Velvet Blossom next week in Atlanta."

"But you don't want to leave the island."

One guess why. It starts with P and ends with -aisley.

"I want you to go in my place. Take Dakota with you. She's smart. She'll charm everyone on the board."

I frown. I don't want Dakota to charm anyone but me. Correction. I don't want Dakota to charm anyone, period.

"You can't continue to be an asshole to her."

"I know. I apologized and gave her a stupid plant."

He chuckles. "Don't sound so resentful."

I'm not resentful. I'm pissed at myself for losing control. I'm famous for my control. But I lost it over a bit of salt in my coffee. It's out of character for me, and I don't like it.

"In the meantime, sit down with Dakota and go over what you expect to happen at the meeting with Velvet Blossom. We need to convince them to continue the deal with a limited supply of whiskey until we can increase production."

"I'll run some numbers and figure out how much whiskey we can supply to their restaurants without pissing off our regular customers."

"Good. I'll expect a banana … er… report in the next day or two."

I narrow my eyes on him. "Not funny."

"Wrong, brother. It was hilarious."

I snarl at him. "Wait until she pranks you."

"I'm not stupid. She's my assistant. I know better than to piss her off."

"I was merely voicing my concerns about her qualifications for the job." I sound like a douchebag.

"Have you seriously learned nothing? Dakota is qualified and she's staying."

"I know. I shouldn't have said anything. I just worry."

He sighs. "I know you do. I know you've protected this family in my absence. Hell, even when I was here, I was too busy working to help Mom pay for rent and food and clothes. I was absent far too often."

"Stop." I hold up a hand. "We're not playing the blame game. We both worked hard to keep this family together. Your contribution was money. Mine was protecting our brothers from bullies and making sure they didn't get into too much trouble."

Eli stares at me for a long moment before nodding. "We good?"

"Always."

"Now get out there and make friendly with my assistant. There's not enough room in the reception area for plants for every one of your fuck ups."

"I don't piss her off that much."

He barks out a laugh. I give him the finger before shutting the door behind me.

I nearly stumble when I notice Dakota leaning against the opposite wall. She waves a set of papers at me.

"Do you want to discuss these numbers now? Or do you want to crawl into your office and think up reasons I shouldn't help on this project?"

I sigh. "Eli told you already?"

"He told me before you went into his office. I'm his right-hand person. I know what he's thinking before he thinks it."

I narrow my eyes on her. "Trying to bag yourself a billionaire?"

She rears back. "No, thank you. I do not want to live in a mausoleum or date a man who wears three-piece suits every day."

"Hey!" Eli shouts from inside his office. "I resemble that remark."

"Besides, everyone on Smuggler's Hideaway knows he's been pining away for Paisley for the past decade," she says in a loud voice.

"I don't pine anymore!" Eli shouts. Not since he and Paisley have gotten together.

"And you don't whine, either."

"Exactly," he says.

"He's a liar," she whispers to me. "He's a great big whiner."

"And I know he was pining for Paisley," I add.

She smiles at me and those green eyes sparkle. My gaze gets caught on her bowtie lips. My fingers itch to pull her into my arms and taste those lips. Does she taste of happiness? I don't know but I want to find out.

I shove my hands in my pockets before I do anything stupid.

"The numbers." She waves the papers again. "Now or later?"

I check my watch. "I can do now."

"Alrighty then. Off we go." She motions with the hand containing the paperwork but she must not have a good grip on them since they scatter onto the floor.

"I've got this," I say as I lean over to collect the sheets.

"My mess. My clean up."

She quickly gathers the papers together. She starts to stand and – bam! – her head whacks into my chin. "Ow," she mutters before falling back on her ass.

I rub my chin. "You're hard-headed."

"Your chin isn't exactly soft either." She massages her head. "That's going to leave a bump."

I bat her hands away. "Let me see."

I dig my hands through her hair and nearly moan at how soft it is. I didn't expect her hair to be this soft, considering how curly it is. It would be entirely too easy to fist her hair and tilt her chin back before devouring her mouth.

My cock jumps. It's down with this idea. I tell it to calm down. She's hurt. Now is not the time to get horny.

I locate the bump and examine it. "It's not very big, but we should ice it before it swells further."

I help her stand. "There's ice in the breakroom."

"I blame your square jaw for this," she mutters as I help her to the breakroom.

"Yes. The incident has nothing to do with your propensity to have accidents."

She gasps. "Accidents! You make it sound as if I'm incontinent."

"I was trying to say you're a klutz without using the word klutz."

"Beep." She feigns hitting a buzzer. "You have failed."

I pull out a chair for her and make sure she's steady before opening the cabinet under the sink. I dig out the first aid kit and rummage around for a cold pack. I squeeze the bag to activate it before shaking it. Once it's cold, I place it in a towel.

"Let me know if it's too cold," I mumble as I place the pack on Dakota's head.

She grimaces. "It's not too cold but it's not pleasant either. Not completely horrible. Maybe a four on the scale of injuries."

I chuckle. "Scale of injuries?"

She shrugs. "I am a bit accident prone."

"Aha! I knew it. My poor jaw has been wrongfully accused."

She wags a finger at me. "Not true. I maintain your square jaw hurt more than a squiggly jaw."

"A squiggly jaw? I would never have a squiggly jaw."

She giggles and the sound fills me with warmth. This woman is amazing. Despite what an asshole I was to her, she's laughing and joking with me. She doesn't put up with my shit.

No wonder I'm drawn to her.

Too bad she's hiding secrets. Secrets destroy lives. I won't allow her to destroy any Raider lives.

Chapter 11

"Is there a limit to how many mess-ups a person can make in one day? Asking for a friend." ~ Dakota

DAKOTA

"Where are you going?" I holler after Rhett when he sails past the end of the line to check in for our flight to Atlanta. "The end of the check-in line is here."

He snorts. "We're not flying economy."

I hurry after him. "But I booked the tickets. And I booked economy."

"And I upgraded our seats to business when I checked us in online."

I blink. He's acting as if flying business is no big deal. Meanwhile, I booked the plane tickets. I nearly had a heart attack at the price for business class seats.

"You upgraded us?"

He shrugs. "It's not a big deal."

Maybe not to him. I've flown exactly twice in my life. Once to Cancun for my honeymoon. And back from Cancun when it ended.

"Come on. I want to get these bags checked in so we can visit the lounge before our flight. I didn't have time to eat lunch."

"The lounge?" I mutter as I trail after him.

There's no line at the business class check-in. And, apparently, there's a different security line for people traveling business class. Who knew?

Within fifteen minutes, we're strolling into a lounge. Or, rather, Rhett is strolling. I'm tiptoeing behind him.

"I shouldn't be in here," I whisper to him.

His brow wrinkles. "Why not?"

I motion to the other people dressed in fancy business suits. Meanwhile, I'm wearing a suit I picked up at a second-hand shop. "I don't belong here."

"You'll be fine." He places a hand on my lower back and ushers me into the lounge.

With him guiding me, I almost feel like I belong. Like I could be one of these people who are confident of their place in the world. Must be nice.

"Do you want anything to eat or drink?"

"Um…" I'm too busy trying to shrink into my chair so no one will notice how I'm not one of them to think about food.

"I'll make you a plate."

He shrugs out of his suit jacket before making his way to the buffet. My gaze snags on the way his ass shifts in his suit pants. And then there's his button-down shirt. It strains to contain his muscles. I never thought a suit could be sexy before. I was wrong.

I'm not the only one who notices. Several women watch him as he makes his way through the buffet. One woman even licks her lips. Another crosses her legs as she bats her eyes toward him.

A pit grows in my stomach. It's stupid. I can't be jealous. Rhett isn't mine to be jealous of. And today is a good reminder of how the man is way out of my league. We're not even in the same division.

He returns and places a plate of food in front of me with a bottle of water.

"How come your plate is three times as big as mine?"

"Because I saw the sandwich you ate for lunch."

My cheeks warm. I ate an extra-large sandwich for lunch because I figured we wouldn't get any food again until we arrive in Atlanta. I had no desire to spend my limited funds on an overpriced sandwich and a bottle of water in the airport. It's bad enough I'm missing two nights of working at the motel for this trip.

Rhett nudges my plate closer to me. "Eat. When we arrive in Atlanta, it's straight into meetings. Who knows when we'll have a chance to eat again."

He doesn't need to tell me twice. I dig into the pasta salad. I moan as the pesto flavor explodes in my mouth. "This is good. They didn't use the pre-made pesto I use."

Rhett's eyes flare as he stares at me.

"What? Did I spill? Oh no. I didn't bring extra clothes. I can't spill."

He clears his throat. "You didn't spill."

"Phew."

I'm not joking. When I accepted the job with Eli, he told me the dress code at the distillery is casual. I bought one suit, just in case. And it's the only suit I have.

Rhett shovels his food into his mouth while I savor mine. This is seriously the best pasta salad I've ever eaten.

When he stands to get seconds, I stop him. "We need to get to the gate."

He checks his watch. "We have forty-five minutes."

"Boarding is in fifteen minutes."

"Plenty of time."

My knee bounces underneath the table as I watch him eat another helping of food. We can't miss our flight. If we miss our flight, we'll miss our meeting. If we miss our meeting, we'll screw up the deal with Velvet Blossom. If we screw up the deal, Eli will fire me.

My chest tightens, and I struggle to breathe. I can't lose this job. The motel gig doesn't offer health insurance. And I can't afford my medicine without health insurance.

Rhett pats my hand. "You okay?"

"Yea. I just don't want to be late," I squeak. I clear my throat and try again. "I hate being late."

"I noticed. You're the first one at the office most mornings. Besides Eli. But he's a machine."

I'm not at the office because I worry about being late. I'm at the office because I worry about falling asleep and the alarm not waking me after working all night. I go straight to the brewery after my night shift to avoid it.

Rhett stands. "Let's go before you have a heart attack."

Thank the food gods. He's finally finished eating.

We walk to the gate and Rhett passes all of the waiting passengers and aims straight for the front.

"What are you doing?" I hiss.

"There's no need to wait."

"Everyone has to wait their turn."

He smirks. "Lucky for us, it's our turn."

"But…"

My words trail off when he scans our boarding passes and the agent motions him forward.

"I don't understand."

"First class passengers never wait," he says.

I screech to a halt. "First class? You said business." Which was bad enough. First class?

He shrugs. "You were freaked out about business class. I figured first class would be worse."

He noticed how I freaked out? He wasn't supposed to notice. And definitely not remark upon it. Party foul! My cheeks warm. I'm probably fifty shades of red now.

I concentrate on the ground and follow him down the jetway to the plane. The flight attendant shows him to his seat. I didn't realize flight attendants showed people to their seats. My previous experience flying involved people shoving past me, elbows being thrown, and a fight for the armrest since I got stuck in a middle seat.

"Do you want the window or the aisle?" Rhett nudges me. "Window or the aisle, Dakota?"

"Can I have the window?" I whisper.

He motions me into the row. "Go for it."

There are only two seats on our side of the aisle. I sit down and nearly moan at the feeling of comfortable leather. Usually, I struggle to fit into the seat, but this one is plenty wide for me.

"Ma'am."

Rhett chuckles. "The flight attendant is talking to you."

"I'm sorry." I blink up at her. "How can I help?"

She hands me a package. "This is your amenity package."

"Amenity package?"

"I love first timers." She hands a package to Rhett before continuing to the other passengers in first class.

I open the package to discover a toothbrush and toothpaste, lotion and lip balm, some perfume, earplugs, an eye mask, and fluffy socks.

"How long is this flight?" I mutter as I go through the items.

Rhett chuckles before handing me a blanket and pillow.

I frown. "Why are you handing me a blanket and pillow?"

"You've yawned three times since we boarded the plane five minutes ago. I figured you'd want to take a nap before we arrive."

"Don't we need to go over the latest numbers?"

He shakes his head. "We're good. Rest."

I open my mouth to protest but yawn instead. He barks out a laugh. "Get some sleep, Dakota. We have a busy two days ahead of us."

No need to tell me three times. I unfurl the blanket and settle myself underneath it. I'm searching for my eye mask when Rhett reaches across me.

"You have to wear your seatbelt, Dakota. You need to be safe."

He clicks my seatbelt in place and tightens the belt before tucking the blanket underneath my chin.

My eyes itch. No one's tucked me in before. Adam certainly didn't when we were married. And before Adam? I prefer not to think about what I missed out on growing up in care.

"Thank you," I manage to say without bawling.

"Sleep well, Dakota."

I glance away and close my eyes before the tears threatening can escape. Who is this man? He doesn't remind me of the Rhett who tried to get me fired. Or the Rhett who threw a coffee mug. Or a controlling man.

This Rhett is a man I could fall in love with.

But you can't, Dakota. He's your brother's boss, and you work with him. Getting involved with someone I work with is a bad idea. Plus, his mood changes quicker than an otter can crawl under my shirt.

It's better to keep my distance.

Chapter 12

"I didn't prepare for this eventuality either." ~ Rhett

RHETT

I squeeze Dakota's shoulder. "Time to wake up, sleepyhead."

She slept through the entire flight – the take-off, meal service, and landing. She didn't fidget or readjust her blanket. She barely moved.

My gaze drifted to her time and time again. Even with those startling green eyes shut, she's a stunner. Except for the dark smudges under her eyes. Is she not getting enough sleep?

"What? Where are we?" She brushes her curls out of her face.

"We're nearly at the gate."

"Gate?" She blinks in confusion a few times before clarity shows in her eyes. "Atlanta. Right."

The seatbelt sign dings off and I stand to remove our carry-ons from the overhead bin before helping her to her feet.

She smooths a hand down her jacket and frowns. "My clothes are all wrinkled."

"No worries. We're checking into the hotel before our first meeting. You have time to change."

Her cheeks darken. "I'll iron these. It'll be fine."

Passengers begin to deboard the plane and I usher her in front of me. There's no sense flying first class if you can't be the first one off the plane.

We make our way through the airport to the baggage claim. I frown when I notice the men taking second glances at Dakota. I glare at a few. She's not theirs to covet.

She's not yours either.

"Oh look." Dakota runs away. "One of our suitcases is already on the belt."

I chase after her. "I'll get it."

But I'm too late. She's already lifting the suitcase from the belt. Or, rather, she's trying to. The suitcase is filled with samples of our whiskey. It's not the lightest.

"I've got it," she hollers, but she doesn't manage to lift the suitcase and ends up running to keep up with the belt as she continues to try and lift it. She trips on air and starts to fall.

I rush after her and manage to catch her before she falls to the ground. "You okay?"

"I'm fine, but the suitcase is getting away."

"It'll come around again."

Her eyes flare and I realize I'm holding her close and rubbing a hand in circles on her lower back. My cock sighs. *Finally.* No, not finally. I clear my throat and step away.

"You stay here." I hand her the carry-ons. "I'll get the suitcases."

I don't give her a chance to respond before walking off. My klutzy girl is stubborn. If she thinks she can help, she will. I have no desire to watch her get dragged by a suitcase over the baggage belt.

I spot the suitcases. I grunt as I grab them from the belt. They're heavy. I can't believe Dakota tried to lift them. She's a little thing. She shouldn't be lifting heavy items.

"Should I order us a ride share?" she asks when I join her. "I didn't order one in advance as they say to wait until you have your luggage."

She pulls out her phone but I stop her. "It's handled."

Her nose wrinkles. "Handled? I'm supposed to be in charge of the travel arrangements."

"No one's keeping score." I motion her forward. "Let's go."

When she appears unsure of where to go, I take the lead. I shorten my stride to make sure she can keep up as we exit the baggage claim area. I scan the area for my name. When I notice a man holding a placard up with my name on it, I aim for him.

"Mr. Raider?" he asks and I nod. "Let me take your bags."

I allow him to take the suitcases before wrestling the carry-ons away from Dakota. And I do mean wrestle. The stubborn woman doesn't let go easily.

"But I'm not carrying anything," she complains as we follow the driver to the car.

"You have your purse."

"A purse doesn't count."

"Is it not a bag?"

"Whatever," she mumbles as we reach the car.

I help the driver situate the bags in the trunk before opening the door for her. She slides in and I follow her.

"I thought you'd go through the other door."

Go through the other door when I can feel Dakota's curves against mine as she scoots to the other side of the seat? I'm not a stupid man.

"Are you feeling better?" I ask once we're driving away from the airport.

"Feeling better? I haven't been sick."

"I didn't say you were. But you were obviously tired."

"I've been reviewing the information for the meeting."

I reach across the seat to squeeze her hand. "There's no reason to be nervous."

She sniffs and lifts her nose in the air. "I know. But I prefer to be prepared for all eventualities."

She's adorable when she's feisty. Whoa. I stop myself there. Dakota is not adorable. Or cute. Or sexy. Or anything.

She's my co-worker, my brother's assistant, and off limits.

My phone rings and I check the display. "It's one of our customers. I need to answer this."

She flicks her hand. "Of course. We're at work."

I spend the rest of the drive trying to iron out the mess of invoices and payments with the customer. Dakota hears me and opens her laptop to bring up the customer files. I grin at her.

I never should have asked Eli to fire her. I overreacted when I found her sleeping in her car. Dakota is not merely competent. She's amazing. As I argue with the customer, she taps on the screen to indicate the numbers I need without me asking. Like I said – amazing.

I finish up the call as the car pulls up to our hotel. I climb out before turning around to help Dakota out. Sparks fly as our hands touch. I could get addicted to the feeling.

Co-worker, I remind myself. Keeping a secret, I add when co-worker does nothing to dim the fire building in my belly to have this woman. To lay her down and feast on her curves. My cock hardens and lengthens as visions of her in the throes of passion flit through my mind.

"Rhett." Dakota elbows me and I realize I'm not paying attention to the present. "Do we tip the driver?"

All the suitcases are already on the porter's cart. I force my thoughts to the present. "Already done."

We follow the porter into the hotel. Dakota gasps and her mouth gapes open as she stares up at the chandelier in the lobby.

It reminds me of when Eli made his first million. He took the entire family on a vacation to the Bahamas where we stayed in a five-star hotel. I don't think my chin lifted from the ground the entire time.

I forgot how wonderful the first experience of luxury is.

I grasp Dakota's elbow and guide her toward the reception. She blinks several times before she slips into work mode.

"We have a reservation for two rooms under the name of Rhett Raider."

The receptionist smiles at her. "Let me have a look."

She taps away at her computer but the smile falls from her face. "I only have one room reserved."

"No. There must be some kind of mistake." Dakota digs her phone out of her purse. "I have a confirmation for two rooms."

The receptionist frowns as she scans Dakota's phone. "I see the confirmation, but I'm not seeing it on my computer."

"It's not a problem. Book us into another room," I say.

The receptionist ticks away at her computer again. "I'm afraid we're completely booked up. The only room we have available is the Empire Suite."

"Sounds expensive," Dakota says.

"It's fine." I hand the receptionist my credit card.

Dakota wrings her hands while the receptionist books the room. But she doesn't speak. She remains mute as the porter escorts us to the elevator and to the top floor of the hotel and when the butler greets us.

"Shall I give you a tour of the suite?" he asks.

"We're good. I'll ring for you if we need anything."

He nods before leaving us alone.

The door closes behind us and I count down – five, four, three—

"This is crazy!" Dakota bursts out. "It's entirely too much money. I should go to another hotel. There must be a hotel nearby that doesn't cost a year's worth of salary to stay in for two nights."

"It's fine."

"Fine!" she yells. "There's a living room, a kitchen, and a freaking gym. In a hotel room."

"Suite," I correct because I'm enjoying watching how flustered Dakota is. Her green eyes spark and her cheeks darken.

I didn't think it was possible for her to be more beautiful than she already is. I was wrong.

"We should go somewhere else. I should go somewhere else."

"I bet you didn't prepare for this eventuality," I poke because I'm having the best time.

Fear fills her eyes. "I really am sorry. I did book two rooms. The receptionist agrees. There must be a glitch in their system. We should have asked to speak to the manager and complained. Please don't complain to Eli."

Damnit. Here I am having fun teasing her, and she's worried about her job. I'm being an asshole. Again. When it comes to Dakota, I can't seem to stop myself from messing up.

I place my hands on her shoulders. She dips her chin to stare at the ground.

"Look at me, Dakota."

She huffs before lifting her gaze to meet mine. Those stunning green eyes are filled with trepidation. Because of me.

"You didn't mess up. And I'm not going to complain to Eli. I promise I won't try to get you fired again. I was wrong to speak to Eli in the first place."

She gulps. "You were?"

"I should have minded my own business."

The fear disappears and the corners of her mouth kick up. "You should have realized how awesome I am from the beginning."

I step away before I kiss the smile clean off of her feisty mouth. Before I glide my hands from her shoulders down her arms to her waist and draw her near.

"Our meeting's in an hour. Do you want to change? I'm going to unpack."

As soon as the words are out, I flee. I'm not a coward. But I've never been good at resisting temptation. And Dakota is temptation in a feisty, stubborn, klutzy package.

Who knew feisty and klutzy were this irresistible?

Chapter 13

"Rhett needs to look up the definition of privacy in the dictionary." ~ Dakota

DAKOTA

I shiver as I fiddle with the thermostat to switch off the air conditioning. It's freezing in this hotel room.

I'm not used to air conditioning. The *Mermaid Motel* doesn't have any. A rickety ceiling fan, I'm convinced is going to fall and decapitate me at some point, is all the cooling off available to me.

I return to my bed and cuddle under the covers. I moan at how soft the linens are. The first thing I'm going to do if I ever pay off Adam's creditors is buy a nice bed with a comfortable mattress and soft sheets.

I yawn. It's been one long ass day. Between flying to Atlanta, the mess up with the room, and a long meeting with the management team of *Velvet Blossom* before an extensive dinner at some fancy restaurant where I had no idea what to do with the thousand forks and knives on the table, I'm exhausted.

But I don't have time to rest. I want to get ahead on some work for Eli so that when I return to Smuggler's Hideaway, I can work fewer hours for a couple days. Sadie's happy to give me more hours at the motel, and considering I'm missing out on two nights of work due to this trip, I want to grab whatever extra hours I can get.

I log into the *Buccaneer's Whiskey* server and get to work. My phone rings but I ignore it. I'm in the middle of a spreadsheet. If I stop now, I'll have to start all over again.

The phone stops ringing and I sigh in relief. My relief isn't long-lived, though, as it immediately begins ringing again. It must be Eli. He can be quite demanding.

"What?" I answer the phone.

"Tsk. Tsk. Tsk. Is that any way to speak to me?"

Crap. It's not Eli. Far from it. It's Grigori. A scary Russian guy my former husband was stupid enough to loan money from.

"What do you want?"

Grigori is scary but I'm not an idiot. If I show him any fear, he'll pressure me even more. He's just an old-fashioned schoolyard bully. With a scar on his neck and a gun in his pocket, but still, the concept's the same.

"I want all the money your husband owes me."

"Dead husband," I correct because I do not want Adam linked to me in the present. The asshole is lucky he's dead and buried.

"What you call him doesn't change anything. You're late."

"I am not late. I have one more day to make the payment."

As soon as I receive my travel allowance from Eli, I'll have enough to pay Grigori. I'm in charge of transferring the travel allowance, so technically I could have paid myself early, but I am not falling into that trap. Pay myself early once and pretty soon I'm paying myself months in advance to get this Russian asshole off my back.

Adam was a scumbag. I am not. Even if I have to deal with scumbags now because of him. Rot in hell, Adam. Rot. In. Hell.

"Banks do not transfer money on Saturdays."

I glance at the calendar and swear under my breath. I forgot tomorrow is Saturday.

"It's not my fault banks don't work on the weekends."

"It's your fault if the money isn't in my account by midnight tomorrow. You know what happens then."

"You can't charge me two-hundred percent interest because the stupid banks are closed."

"Those are the terms agreed upon."

"I didn't agree to those terms!"

"But you'll pay, or do you prefer to suffer the consequences when you don't pay?"

"I can't pay off the debt if I'm dead."

He chuckles. The hairs on my neck rise at the evil sound. "My darling, I don't unalive people. I show them the error of their ways."

I should probably be recording this to send to the police. Hell, I probably should have gone to the police the first time Grigori contacted me. But a dead snake on my dining room table combined with a creepy message was enough to warn me off.

"You'll get your stupid money. Now, leave me alone." I end the call and throw the phone on the bed.

"Who was on the phone?"

"Aaargh!" I scream and clutch my chest.

Rhett raises his hands in the air. "I didn't mean to frighten you."

"For someone who doesn't mean to frighten me, you scare the devil out of me often enough."

"Who was on the phone?"

I glare at him. "Were you eavesdropping on my conversation?"

"You weren't being quiet."

"The volume of my voice is not an excuse to eavesdrop on my conversation."

He shrugs. "Regardless. I heard you."

I feel my cheeks heat, but I ignore my embarrassment. I'm not the one who should be embarrassed. Rhett should be embarrassed for violating my privacy.

"Be a gentleman and pretend you didn't."

He crosses his arms over his chest. I force my gaze to remain on his face. I will not check out those muscles. No, siree bob. Not me.

"A gentleman doesn't let a lady suffer."

"Lucky for you, I'm no lady."

"Dakota," he grumbles.

I lower my voice and imitate him. "Rhett."

"I can stand here all night."

"This is my room."

He nods to the doorway. "Which I'm not standing in."

Why the hell didn't I shut my door? No use worrying about it now. I'll simply rectify the situation.

I slam my laptop shut and fling the covers off of me before marching to the door. I try to shut it, but Rhett sticks his foot in the jam to stop me.

"What the hell are you wearing?" he grumbles in a low voice, which I absolutely one-hundred percent refuse to believe is sexy.

"Pajamas. It's what normal people wear to bed."

His brow lifts. "Normal people do not wear those."

I grunt. If I had known I was going to share a suite with Rhett, I would have packed my flannel pajamas. But I didn't. And now I'm in a tiny tank top and matching shorts. See the aforementioned comment regarding the fan determined to behead me.

I slap my hand on the door. "Let me shut the door and then you don't have to see my abnormal pajamas."

He frowns. "I'm not going away until you explain who you were talking to on the phone."

"I'll tell you." I lean close. "None. Of. Your. Business."

He growls.

"It's called privacy for a reason, Mr. High and Mighty."

"I'm not letting you use privacy as an excuse to hide secrets from me."

I rear back. "Hide secrets from you? Who do you think I am? Your best friend? Are we going to braid each other's hair next?"

"Stop trying to distract me."

I push up on my toes and get in his face. "Stop invading my privacy."

"If you don't tell me what's wrong, I can't help you."

"Who said I need your help? Do I resemble a woman who can't help herself?"

His gaze rakes my body and he coughs. "I didn't say you're helpless. I said I could help."

"Wake up and smell the fire. I don't need your help."

"Oh yeah?" He cocks a brow. "Prove it."

"I don't need to prove anything to you. I'm not one of your brothers who enjoys accepting dares and spending days in bed with poison ivy on their junk." I hold up a hand. "And please don't ever tell me what happened. I do not want to know."

His eyes narrow and I can practically see his mind spinning around over different ideas. When he smirks, I know I'm in trouble. And not the good kind either.

"I'll tell Eli."

Ice settles in my veins. I can't lose this job. I'll have to flee. Grigori knows where I am. "You'll tell Eli what? You have no idea what's happening."

"Who do you owe money to?"

Crap. He does have an idea what's happening.

"None of your business."

"Don't make me tell Eli."

"Don't blame being a tattletale on me. If you tell Eli, that's on you. Not me."

"Dammit Dakota, tell me what's going on. I can't help you if I'm in the dark."

I throw my arms in the air. "I don't need you to help me. I can pay my debts without Mr. High and Mighty helping me."

"Do not call me Mr. High and Mighty," he grumbles.

"Mr. High and Mighty. Mr. High and Mighty. Mr. High and Mighty."

He growls before palming my neck and drawing me near. I slam into his body. He melds his lips to mine and I immediately realize I messed up. Because now I want more.

But I shouldn't. I should know better. Men are assholes who will lie, cheat, and steal to get what they want. All while pretending to love you to your face.

No thanks.

"Let me in," Rhett whispers against my lips and my panties dampen at the feel of his rumbling voice against my mouth.

Shit. I am in so much trouble.

Chapter 14

"Dakota is havoc on my control." ~ Rhett

RHETT

"Let me in," I demand.

Dakota moans before opening. I don't hesitate. I dive in. She tastes of strawberries and sin. Damn. I fucked up.

I was barely hanging on to my control before I tasted her. But now I know how she tastes, how she moans when I touch her, how she presses herself against me to get closer, and my control is shattering.

I dig my fingers into her hair and use the hold to yank her head back. I trace kisses along her jaw until I reach her ear.

"Tell me no," I growl into her ear.

"W-w-what?" She stutters.

"Tell me no. I have no control when it comes to you. Tell me no, or I'm going to throw you on this bed and have my wicked way with you."

"Does wicked way include me having an orgasm?"

I nip her bottom lip. "More than one."

Her eyes flare. "More than one?"

I groan. "Tell me no, Havoc."

"Havoc?"

"You came into my life and turned it upside down, Havoc." She smirks and I tug on her hair. "Tell me no."

"Why do you want me to say no?"

"Because I have no control when it comes to you. I will take and take from you until I wring every orgasm out of your body I can."

I feel her chest move up and down against mine as her breathing quickens. "If you want me to say no, you need to stop promising to give me multiple orgasms."

"Oh, Havoc, I'll give you as many orgasms as you want."

"I've never had more than one orgasm during sex before."

I freeze. "What?"

Her cheeks darken. "Don't make me say those words again. They were embarrassing enough the first time I said them."

"No." I pinch her chin. "You shouldn't be embarrassed. The men who weren't able to pleasure you should be embarrassed."

I didn't think it was possible, but her face darkens further. "Man," she squeaks.

"Sorry?"

"Man." She glances away. "I've only been with one man."

My cock presses against my zipper. It's ready to show Dakota how good sex can be. To prove to her one orgasm is the minimum.

"Tell me no."

Her brow wrinkles. "If you don't want to have sex with me, walk away."

"You don't get it. My control is about to snap."

She studies me, and her eyes grow calculating before she steps back. I drop my hold on her. She's saying no. This is what I wanted I remind myself while my cock swears at me.

"I'll…"

My words trail off when she grasps the hem of her tank top and whips it over her head, baring her chest to me. I nearly swallow my tongue. Dakota's breasts are round and full – more than a handful.

My mouth waters. I want to explore with my lips and tongue, and hands. As I stare, her nipples harden. I moan. I haven't touched her, and she's already responsive to me. I can't wait to see what happens when I do touch her soft skin.

"Yes. I say—"

She doesn't get a chance to finish before I'm on her. I circle her hips and lift her up until her breasts are level with my mouth. She grasps my shoulders to steady herself and I latch onto one of her pretty pink nipples. She arches into me and I hurry to set her on the bed before we tip over.

"Hands on the headboard."

"But I want to touch you," she pouts.

"If you touch me, I'll be rutting into you like a damn animal in heat."

She giggles. "I don't think male animals go into heat."

"If you want me to give you more than one orgasm, you need to listen to my orders, Havoc."

Her eyes flare before she narrows them. "Mr. High and Mighty has arrived at the party."

"Sass me and I won't give you any."

She bites her bottom lip as she gazes up at me from beneath her lashes. "I reserve the right to sass you if you don't give me at least two orgasms."

"Challenge accepted," I mutter before grasping her shorts and yanking them down her legs, leaving her lying naked before me. "You weren't wearing panties."

"I don't wear panties to bed."

My cock twitches. It likes the idea of imagining our little havoc laying in bed without panties on.

"Hands on the headboard," I order.

She stares at me as she slowly lifts her arms and grabs the headboard. The motion causes her breasts to jut forward. Fucking magnificent.

I draw a finger around her nipple. Her skin pebbles in response. Fucking magnificent.

"I love how sensitive your breasts are," I mutter as I begin to knead and massage them.

I latch onto a nipple and swirl my tongue around it. Dakota moans before wrapping her legs around my waist.

I continue to tease her breasts as she rubs her naked core against my jeans-clad cock. My cock presses against my zipper. I'm going to have a zipper imprint, but I don't dare remove my clothes. I won't be able to resist sinking into her once I'm naked and she needs to come first.

I grasp a thigh with my free hand. "Legs on the bed."

She whimpers.

"Don't worry. I'll give you what you need."

She drops her legs.

"Good girl."

I caress her thigh. "Widen your legs for me."

She doesn't hesitate to follow my directions. There's a first for everything.

I glide my fingers up her inner thigh, careful not to touch her core before reversing direction. I love how smooth her skin is. I could worship her curves for days.

She grunts.

"Is there something you want, Havoc?"

She squirms. "You know what I want."

I blink up at her. "I do?"

She glares at me. "You promised me orgasms."

"Don't worry. You'll come more than once tonight."

She lifts her brows. "Tonight?"

I chuckle. "Are you impatient?"

"I've never had more than one orgasm before. Wouldn't you be impatient?"

At the reminder of being the second man to pleasure her, I nearly lose my control. My cock pulses and my fingers itch to dive into her pussy to discover how warm and wet she is.

"You're making it difficult for me to be gentle," I grit out.

"Who asked for gentle? It must have been some other woman because it wasn't me."

I growl. I don't want any other women. I want Dakota. No matter how much havoc she causes in my life. I want her.

Crap. I can't let Dakota in. I need to protect the family from her. Except… I discovered her secrets tonight. Maybe I can take a chance on this woman.

I force those thoughts away. I'm not contemplating the future now. Right now, I'm going to make Dakota come so many times she forgets all about the asshole before me.

I tease her opening with my finger. "Is this what you want?"

"Y-y-yes."

"Or maybe this?" I circle her clit and she moans.

"Or is it both?" I inch one finger into her pussy while pressing my palm against her clit. Fuck. She feels better than I could have ever imagined. Let me in, my cock pleas.

I begin to pump my fingers into her and she lifts her hips to meet my thrusts.

"Has any man made you feel this good before?" I ask as I add another finger.

"No," she gasps.

"Do you want any other man to make you feel this good?"

I regret the question the second it leaves my lips – I shouldn't be making promises about the future together – but I can't help myself. I have no control with Dakota. I want things from her I shouldn't want. I can't trust her, and without trust, there's no chance for us.

"No."

"Do you want to come for me?"

Her walls flutter around my fingers and I press my palm harder against her clit.

"Yes."

I use my free hand to massage her breast. "Are you going to come for me?"

"Yes."

"Then, come." I tweak her nipple and she explodes. Her mouth drops open in a silent scream as her back arches off the bed and her pussy pulses around my fingers.

"There you go, Havoc. Take what you need," I murmur as I continue to pump into her until her climax wanes.

She collapses on the bed and her eyes slowly open. "Holy shit."

I smirk. "We're just getting started."

I lick her taste off of my fingers and moan. "My Havoc tastes of strawberries and sin."

Her eyes flare as she watches me.

"Do you want me to make you come with my mouth?"

She bites her lip as she contemplates her answer. "Maybe later."

Thank fuck. There's no way I can taste her without coming in my goddamn jeans like a teenaged boy.

Speaking of which. I roll off the bed and whip my t-shirt off. Dakota licks her lips as she watches me.

"Keep staring at me like you want to eat me and this won't last very long."

"You promised me multiple orgasms," she sasses.

She's going to be the death of me. I grab a condom from my back pocket – I refuse to think about why I put it there in the first place – before shoving my jeans down my legs.

My fingers tremble as I don the condom. I inhale a deep breath and reach for the control I'm famous for. I want to make this good for Dakota. I want her addicted to me. I want her to forget all about the asshat who didn't know how to pleasure her. She should be obsessed with me. Think about me when she's by herself. Not him. Me.

Damnit. Those are not the thoughts of a man in control.

I clear my throat and climb back on the bed with Dakota. I notch my cock at her entrance.

"Let me know if anything I do is too much."

I wait for her nod before sinking into her. She feels better than anyone before her. I could become obsessed with her. With making her come. With watching her breasts jiggle as I pound into her.

Those are dangerous thoughts. I cut them off. I can't trust Dakota. Without trust, there's no way forward for us. This is a one-off occasion. Nothing more.

Chapter 15

"Ah, regret, my old friend has arrived to taunt me." ~
Dakota

DAKOTA

I stretch my legs as I slowly wake. These sheets feel fabulous against my naked skin. Whoa! Naked skin. Why am I naked?

The arm around my waist tightens and memories assault me. Rhett touching my skin. Rhett sinking into me. Rhett making me come more times than I can count.

Sex with Adam was never this good. Not even in the beginning, before his 'work' trips began. I can't wait for the next time.

Next time? Slow your roll, Dakota. There won't be a next time.

Rhett made himself perfectly clear. Last night was a one and done situation. Although, the one turned into several times, as evidenced by the delicious ache in my core.

I guess I shouldn't be annoyed he eavesdropped on my conversation, or else— Hold on. Rhett only had sex with me after he overheard my conversation with Grigori. Oh no. Did he have pity sex with me?

I need to get out of here. I can't handle the brush off. Not from Rhett.

I've been here before. I thought we were becoming friends when we huddled together in a closet during a hurricane but Rhett couldn't wait to point out how wrong I was.

I bite my inner cheek before I groan at how stupid I was last night. But who can blame me? Rhett Raider is the sexiest man I've ever met. One of the sexiest men on Smuggler's Hideaway. When he promised me multiple orgasms, I couldn't resist.

But I won't be a fool twice.

Especially since being a fool last night may well lead to the end of my career at *Buccaneer's Whiskey*. Eli wouldn't listen to Rhett before but maybe he will now, since Rhett can prove how unprofessional I acted.

My body tingles with the need to escape. To pretend last night never happened.

I lift Rhett's arm and scooch until I'm at the edge of the bed. I place a pillow under his arm and he cuddles it with a sigh.

I snatch my phone from the nightstand before tiptoeing to the bathroom. I shut the door behind me and open the app for the airline. I change my flight to one leaving in ninety minutes. I need to hurry.

Lucky for me, this fancy hotel suite has a walk-in closet attached to the bathroom. I don't bother with a shower. I throw on some clothes and shove everything back into my carry-on.

I place my ear against the door and listen for any sign of movement from Rhett. When I don't hear anything, I slowly open the door and peek out. He's fast asleep and facing away from me. Now's my chance.

I carry my bag out of the room and creep toward the front door. I snag my purse from the counter and grab my shoes before leaving. When the door clicks shut, I can breathe for the first time this morning. I made it.

I check the time on my phone. Not quite. I need to catch my earlier flight before I can rule this escape a success.

I hurry to the elevator. When I'm inside, I kneel down to put on my shoes. The door opens on another floor and a couple enters. Her eyes widen when she notices me putting my shoes on. Oh god. Is this what a walk of shame is?

My cheeks heat. "I slept in. I have a flight in just over an hour. I don't want to miss it," I ramble.

The woman grins. "Ah, to be young again."

Apparently, I'm not fooling her one bit.

We arrive at the lobby and I shoot out of the elevator. I ignore the reception. Rhett can deal with checking us out. I have a plane to catch and an escape to complete.

I skid to a halt in front of the doorman.

"I need a taxi to the airport."

"Of course, ma'am."

He takes my bag and leads me outside, where a row of taxis are waiting. Oh. Silly me. I forgot we're staying at a fancy schmancy hotel.

The driver of the first taxi jumps out of his car to open the trunk.

I fidget as the doorman and driver secure my suitcase. Do I tip the doorman? How much?

The doorman smiles at me. "Mr. Raider will settle up with me."

My shoulders sag in relief. I should probably be embarrassed – again – that my nervousness is obvious to one and all, but I can't bother to care now. I need out of here.

As we drive to the airport, I watch the taxi meter with alarm. The dollars add up faster than I can count and I can count pretty darn fast. I check the bills in my wallet. Luckily, I have a bit more cash than normal on me due to this trip.

When he pulls up to the terminal at the airport, relief fills me. If I only tip ten percent, I have enough cash.

"Sorry," I say as I hand him the money. "I don't usually carry cash."

He pats my arm. "It's okay, honey. Be safe."

Why is everyone being nice to me this morning? Does my face have a sign with 'pathetic loser' on it?

I hurry toward the check-in line and show the attendant my ticket.

"You're in the wrong line."

Panic hits me hard. I need to get on this flight. "I changed my ticket," I explain. "I'm taking an earlier flight."

She points to a different line. "You have a first class ticket. You can check in there."

Relief flits through me. I can still make this flight. "Oh."

"No bags to check in?" the attendant at the first class check-in asks me when I hand her my identification.

Oh no! I left Rhett to handle all of the bags. We had two heavy suitcases filled with various Buccaneer's Whiskeys. I'm such a jerk. I should have at least taken one of them.

"No bags?" the attendant repeats.

I shake my head. "Nothing."

She hands me my boarding pass. "Have a nice flight."

I make my way through security and rush toward the gate. I arrive as the flight is boarding. I start to join the line but I might as well enjoy the privilege of first class since I doubt I'll ever fly first class again.

"Good morning," the flight attendant greets me.

I force a smile. Judging by the way her eyes widen, my smile is more of a grimace.

She leads me to my seat. First class is empty besides me. Good. I can freak out about losing my job in peace.

I'm settling into my seat when she returns with an amenity kit. "You might want to freshen up."

She doesn't give me a chance to ask any questions before she's gone. But now I'm curious. I make my way to the restroom and lock the door behind me. When I gaze into the mirror, I nearly scream. No wonder everyone's being nice to me. I have mascara smudged all over my face and my hair resembles a rat's nest.

Note to self. When you're escaping a one-night stand, wash your face and brush your hair before leaving your hotel room.

I snort. As if I'm ever going to have another one-night stand. In fact, I think I'll return to my previous policy regarding men. Avoid them at all costs.

I scrub my face until it's clean. Then, I tackle my hair. The free brush and comb in the amenity kit are no match for my curls. I finally give up and pile my hair on top of my head. There. I no longer resemble a raccoon.

I return to my seat and settle in for the flight.

The same flight attendant arrives with a glass of champagne. "You look like you could use this."

I don't usually drink, but I'm making an exception today. "You have no idea."

She giggles. "I have some idea. I was young once, too."

"But were you an idiot who slept with your boss's brother, who you also happen to work for? And who hates you?"

I nearly slap a hand over my mouth. Talk about oversharing.

"I'll bring you the bottle," she says before whirling around and marching to the galley.

She's back in less than a minute with a bottle of champagne and some nuts. "I'll serve breakfast once we're in the air but you shouldn't drink on an empty stomach."

I blink back tears at her kindness. "Thank you."

"No need to thank me. Us women need to stick together."

Once she's gone, the tears slip from my eyes. I wipe them away and reach for my glass. I'm not going to worry about the consequences of last night now. No one can phone me while I'm flying. I'll enjoy being unreachable for a few hours and hope my life doesn't implode when I return to Smuggler's Hideaway.

I down the champagne and reach for the bottle.

Chapter 16

"I'm not letting Dakota run from me." ~ Rhett

RHETT

I reach for Dakota and meet air. "Dakota?"

When she doesn't answer, I open my eyes to discover she isn't in the bed. Guessing by how cold the sheets are, she hasn't been for a while.

"Dakota?" I holler again.

I climb out of bed to search for her. The bathroom door is ajar. I peek inside. She's not in there. I turn away but notice her bag is missing from the closet. I swear underneath my breath. I can't believe she fled.

Hold on. We still have a plane to catch. She couldn't have gone far. A quick call to the airline confirms she switched her reservation to an earlier flight.

I growl. She's running from me.

I should probably let her go. But my stomach sinks to the floor at the idea. I don't want to let her go. And, after last night, I don't need to. Not after I found out what secrets she's keeping.

But why is she running from me?

I will find out. I pack up all of my things, plus the suitcases with the samples we brought for *Velvet Blossom* to try. We concluded our business with them a day early. I had planned to spend today showing Dakota Atlanta, but she shot those plans to shit.

I smile at the receptionist when I reach the desk to check out. "I'm checking out a day early."

The receptionist doesn't smile in return. She keeps her gaze focused on the computer.

"Here you are." She slaps the invoice down on the counter.

I don't bother to review it. "It's fine," I say and hand her my credit card.

She swipes it and hands it back to me. "Your payment is successful."

"Have a nice day."

She grunts at me. Someone is not in a good mood this morning. I don't say anything since I'm not a happy camper now either.

"I need help with my bags," I say when the porter doesn't come over to assist me.

She motions for him to help. The man scowls at me as he walks over. Is everyone in Atlanta grumpy this morning?

I follow as the porter rolls my bags to a waiting taxi. When I try to tip him for his help, he holds up a hand.

"No, thank you."

I frown. "Is something wrong?"

"Why don't you ask the lovely lady you kicked out of your hotel room this morning?"

"I didn't…" I don't get a chance to explain before he's gone.

Damnit. What kind of state was Dakota in when she left?

Time crawls by as I travel to the airport, wait for my flight, and fly back home. Worry for Dakota pounds at me as I drive back to Smuggler's Hideaway. I phone Eli.

"Is Dakota at the office?" I ask.

"Why would she be at the office? Aren't you supposed to be in Atlanta for another day?"

"We concluded our business early."

"Didn't Dakota fly home with you?"

"She took an earlier flight."

He groans. "What did you do to her?"

Nothing except taste and touch her all night long. My cock springs to life as the memories assail me.

"Nothing," I croak out.

"If she quits because you were being an asshole, I'm firing your ass."

"You can't fire me. I'm your brother."

"Try me."

I palm my neck and squeeze as I search for calm. Getting into a fight with my brother will not help resolve things now.

"Can you message me Dakota's address?"

"Why?"

"I have some of her things with me." The lie rolls off my tongue.

"I'll message it but do not mess with my assistant. I'm not kidding, Rhett. She's the best assistant I've ever had. I won't lose her because you're an asshole who goes into over-protective mode whenever anyone comes close to the family."

"Thanks." I ring off before Eli asks any more questions.

My phone beeps with a message and I hit a button on my console to read the address. It's a street near the downtown of Smuggler's Rest. I drive to the address. This can't be right.

I'm at the *Mermaid Motel.* Dakota can't possibly live here. But I spot her piece of shit car in the back of the lot. What is she doing here?

I park in front of the reception and march inside to investigate. The bell above the door chimes when I enter and the receptionist glances over with a smile on her face. Her smile disappears when she realizes it's me.

"What the hell are you doing here, Dakota?"

"Um...I...Do I hear the phone?" She whirls around and runs toward the office but slams into the wall instead.

I rush to catch her before she falls. She bats my arms away. "I'm fine."

I lift a brow. "But the wall came out to attack you?"

"Yes." She nods. "Exactly."

I step closer to crowd her and her eyes flare before she clears her throat and glances away. "What are you doing here, Havoc?" She doesn't answer and I continue to push her. "Do you work here?"

"It's none of your business."

"Wrong." I tuck one of her curls behind her ear. "Everything about you is my business."

She scowls. "Stop trying to control me."

"I'm not trying to control you. Wanting to know everything about you, isn't controlling you."

She rolls her eyes. "You don't want to know everything about me."

"Yes, I do, Havoc. Every single thing there is to know."

The bell over the door chimes again. "Ay caramba!" A woman shouts. "Hot. Hot. Hot."

"Who are you?" I ask her.

Dakota pushes past me. "Don't be rude. This is Sadie. She's the manager of the motel."

Sadie bows. "Manager and bringer of caffeine goodness at your service."

She holds up a cup of coffee from *Pirates Pastries* and Dakota snatches it from her.

"Thank you," Dakota mutters before downing half of the cup in one go.

"Thank you," Sadie says as she rounds the receptionist desk to stand behind it. "I was going to lose my mind if I didn't get out of here for an hour. Thanks for covering for me. You can go now."

My brow wrinkles. "You don't work here?" I ask Dakota.

"She works the night shift," Sadie answers and Dakota glares at her.

"What?" Sadie widens her eyes. "It's not a secret. Everyone in town knows."

I don't. Unlike my brothers, I've ignored the Smuggler's Hideaway rumor mill ever since Dad left us. The rumors people spread about what happened to our family turned me off small town gossip forever. While we were trying to survive, the islanders couldn't stop speculating about the woman my dad left his family for.

"Come on." I hold out my hand to Dakota. "We should discuss this in a more private location."

Sadie waggles her eyebrows. "Good thing Dakota lives here."

Dakota throws her arms in the air. "Give away all my secrets now, why don't you?"

Sadie bites her bottom lip. "I'm sorry. I didn't know it was a secret."

Dakota sighs. "I should be the one apologizing. I'm being a brat."

"Brats should be spanked." Sadie winks at me. "Now, get out of here. I have work to do."

I place my hand on Dakota's lower back to escort her out of the motel. I don't miss the way she shivers in response. But I'm not a complete idiot. I keep my mouth shut.

As soon as we're outside, she whirls around on me and retreats a few steps. "I'll see you at work tomorrow."

I chuckle. "Nice try. You aren't running away from me. Again."

Her shoulders slump and guilt tries to worm its way into my consciousness. I ignore it. I have nothing to feel guilty about. Dakota's the one who ran off on me without an explanation.

"Do you want to stand out here and discuss our private business?"

Her eyes narrow on me. "No."

I lift a brow and wait. She grunts before stomping away from me. I enjoy how her ass jiggles as she walks for a while before rushing to catch up to her.

She unlocks a door marked 'owner's suite' and I follow her inside. I scan the room and frown. The suite is dated with worn carpets, cracked countertops, and over-used furniture.

"You live here?"

"Don't you dare make fun of my home."

I hold up my hands. "I wasn't going to."

"Not everyone is a millionaire." She pokes me in the chest and I capture her hand.

"I know, Havoc." I place her hand against my heart and hold it there. "What I don't know is why you ran from me."

"Ran from you?" She yanks her hand away. "What difference does it make?"

"What difference does it make?"

"Yes." She nods. "What difference does it make? The last time I thought we were becoming friendly, you reminded me the next day about how we weren't friends. There's no need to send a message this time. I get it."

"You don't get anything," I grumble. "We're more than friends."

"Just because we had sex doesn't mean anything changed."

"Wrong. Everything changed."

She shakes her head. "Not for me."

I approach her and she retreats until her back hits the wall. I plant my hands on the wall on either side of her. Her breath quickens, and her eyes flare in response to my proximity.

"Everything changed. I know you feel this connection between us, too."

"It doesn't matter what I feel. It's too risky. You could get me fired. I'm not letting a man ruin my life again."

"A man ruined your life? Who? How?"

She ducks her chin. "Never mind."

I pinch her chin and lift until her gaze meets mine. Her green eyes are filled with pain. I can't bear to see her in pain.

"Tell me everything."

Chapter 17

"You don't have the right to know everything about me." ~ Dakota

Dakota

Rhett's lost his mind if he thinks I'm going to tell him everything. I don't owe him an explanation about my life. I don't owe him anything.

"Havoc," he pleads and I nearly get lost in those stunning blue eyes. It should be against the law for a man's eyes to be this captivating. "I don't want to ruin your life. I want to make it better."

When I hesitate, he continues, "If we're going to be in a relationship, you're going to have to tell me at some point."

"Relationship?" My brow wrinkles. "We're not in a relationship."

"Havoc, I've been inside you. I've made you come more times than any man before me."

My cheeks warm. I never should have told him how lacking my earlier sexual encounters have been.

"Sex doesn't make a relationship."

"Last night was more than sex and you know it."

I do? I'm not exactly an expert at understanding the games men and women play. Thus, my living in this outdated suite and working two jobs to pay back debts my previous man racked up.

He caresses my cheek with his thumb. I want to lean into him. Accept the comfort he's freely giving. But I can't. I can't make the same mistakes I've made before.

"You hated me two days ago," I remind him.

"I never hated you."

"You tried to get me fired, and you threatened to tell Eli about my phone call last night."

He grimaces. "I never would have told Eli about the phone call, but am I an asshole for threatening to? Yes."

"At least you understand it was an asshole move."

"Make no mistake about it, Havoc. I will do everything in my power to keep the people I care for safe. Including making threats and rushing home after they ran away from me."

My heart thumps in my chest. People he cares about? He can't care about me.

I don't trust his words. Men lie. Especially when they want something from you. Adam is a prime example.

I need to end this. I need to push him away. I can't trust him. Considering what I feel for him is bigger than anything I ever felt for Adam, I need this to end before he breaks my heart. And he will break my heart. There's no other option.

There's one surefire way to end this. Throw my pride away and expose my idiocy.

"I was married."

His brow wrinkles. "You're divorced?"

"Widowed."

His eyes fill with sympathy. "I'm sorry."

"Don't be. Adam was a liar, a womanizer, and a compulsive gambler."

"What did—"

I hold up my hand to quiet him. "I won't be taking any questions."

He nods. "Continue."

I can't continue when all I can see and smell is Rhett. I shove away from the wall and duck under his arm. I pace the room as I tell my story.

"I met Adam when I was still in care. I fell head over heels for him. He was charming and sweet, and he'd been in care, so he understood me."

Rhett growls, and I narrow my eyes at him. He coughs. "Sorry."

"When I aged out of care, I moved in with him. I worked two jobs while I put myself through community college. We were saving our money to buy a house. I've always wanted to own a house. A home no one can kick me out of. A place with room for my own things. More things than can fit in a black garbage bag."

I stop to stare out of the window at the parking lot. This is not the home I dreamed of. An outdated suite in a rundown motel with a view of parked cars.

"When we signed the papers for our house, I thought I'd won at life. I had a good job managing a plumbing company." I glare at him. "And managing a plumbing company is a good job."

He holds up his hands. "I was an asshole."

Yes, he was. But discussing his past behavior is not on the current agenda.

"Life was good. I thought. Sure, Adam was gone a lot of weekends for work but I didn't mind. I had my home. A place where I felt safe. I spent endless hours shopping at second hand stores for furniture. I even took a class in upselling used items. I didn't sell them, though. I kept them."

I blow out a breath. I don't want to tell the rest of the story. The part when it becomes clear what an idiot I was.

Rhett wraps his arms around me from behind. "Finish it. Rip it off like a Band-Aid. After today, we don't need to discuss this ever again."

"Adam wasn't away for work all those weekends. He was in Atlantic City gambling and paying for hookers."

Rhett growls, but I don't have the emotional bandwidth to comfort him. I'm too lost in my own version of hell.

"The worst part is I didn't know. I had no clue. Until Adam was killed in a car crash. Then, everything fell apart. He wasn't making payments on the mortgage and I lost my home." Tears well in my eyes but I sniff and suck them back up. I've cried enough tears. They don't change anything.

"I managed to consolidate all of his debts for the cars and the house. I thought I had everything covered."

"And then Grigori showed up," Rhett grumbles.

I nod. "I tried to ignore him. But loan sharks refuse to be ignored. A dead snake with a sign 'Next time, it's your turn' was enough to get my attention."

I shiver as I recall walking into the apartment I moved into after I lost my home to discover the snake on the kitchen table.

"There was no way I could keep up with the bank payments and payments to Grigori unless I found a better paying job. When Eli offered me the job as his PA, I couldn't say yes quick enough."

"But your salary isn't enough to pay off the creditors and Grigori?" Rhett asks.

I shrug. "If I don't pay Grigori off fast enough, I'll never get out from under the debt. He compounds the interest over and over again until you end up paying until your death."

"I'll pay off the debt."

I whirl around. "You are not paying off my dead husband's debt."

"What if I loan you the money?"

"No, this is my mess to deal with."

"No," he growls. "This is your husband's mess you got stuck with."

"It doesn't matter how you frame it. I'm the one responsible for paying."

"Why? What's wrong with letting someone help you?"

Because people who help you, think they own you. I can't count the number of times Adam reminded me how I owed him since he let me move in with him when I was eighteen. I ignored him since I thought I loved him. I was a fool.

"I can handle this on my own."

"But you're not on your own."

"Yes, I am."

He palms my neck. "No, you're not. You have me."

I shove on his shoulders until he releases me. "I don't have you. You're my boss's brother who I had sex with."

He growls. "I'm more than Eli's brother. I'm the man you're involved with."

I roll my eyes. "We're not involved. We're not in a relationship."

"Why not?"

My head rears back. "What do you mean, why not? Because we're not. Because you hate me. Because you've tried to have me fired. Because—"

My words are cut off when he slams his lips to mine. I wish I could say I resisted him. Shoved him away and stomped off. But I can't.

I melt into Rhett. I sigh at the feel of his lips against mine. At his clean scent surrounding me, making me feel cherished and safe.

Safe?

I can't trust a man. Look at what happened the last time I did. Good reminder. I shove him away and retreat a few steps.

Rhett sighs. "I admit I pushed you away because I knew you were hiding secrets, but you're not hiding secrets from me anymore."

"You don't know everything about me."

"I'll learn as our relationship grows."

I grit my teeth. "You're not listening to me. We're not in a relationship."

He smirks. "Not yet. I'll convince you to give me a chance."

"No, you won't. I've got a lot on my plate. I don't have time for another thing."

"We'll make time."

"Are you trying to give me a stroke?"

He chuckles. "My Havoc is stubborn."

"I'm not your anything."

He smirks. "I'll change your mind." He saunters to the door. "Get some sleep. I'll see you tomorrow. Lock up behind me."

"You won't change my mind," I holler after him.

He waves in response. I slam my door. Rhett as Mr. High and Mighty was annoying. I'm afraid Rhett 'I'll change your mind' is going to be worse.

But I have to resist him. I don't trust myself to make good choices about men. Look what happened with Adam.

If I lose my job because a relationship with Rhett doesn't work out, what then? Where will I go?

And it's not only my job I'm worried about. I'm afraid my heart won't remain unscathed either.

Chapter 18

"The door attacked me without provocation." ~
Dakota

DAKOTA

I wave to Blossom as I walk toward her. We're going to spend the day together enjoying the *Ghost Tide Festival.* I have no idea what you do at a *Ghost Tide Festival,* but it's going to be an awesome day, no matter what happens, since I have a day off from catering to Eli's whims and from helping drunk guests figure out how to open doors.

"This is so exciting." She bounces on her toes. "I love all things ghost."

"You do?"

"Halloween is my favorite."

I nearly slap my forehead. Duh. *Ghost* tide. Halloween. How did I not connect the two? I blame a lack of sleep from working two jobs. Not lack of sleep from spending way too much time reliving a certain night in a certain hotel room with a certain sexy boss's brother.

"What do you want to do first?"

"I have it all figured out. We'll begin our day at the *Ghost Tide Market*. They're supposed to have all the best goodies. Then, we'll do *The Smuggler's Gauntlet*."

A gauntlet doesn't make me feel all tingly with excitement. Quite the opposite. "The what?"

"Don't worry. It'll be fun."

Her smirk does not reassure me.

"And we'll finish the day off with the *Haunted Cove Boat Ride*."

I shiver. "It sounds scary."

"I know. Isn't it great?"

I shrug. Scary isn't usually my thing, but I'm willing to try anything once.

We walk to the boardwalk where the *Ghost Tide Market* is set up. I shiver as the cold wind off of the ocean hits us. I didn't consider cold ocean breezes when I dressed for the day.

"Oh look. Parker has a stand." Blossom drags me to the *Pirates Pastries* stand.

I inhale the scent of chocolate and cinnamon, and coffee. I moan. "I think I'm in love with you, Parker."

She giggles. "Do you want anything to eat with your coffee?"

"How do you know I'm going to order coffee?" She cocks an eyebrow. "Fine. I'll have a coffee and a..." I scan her offerings. "What's in a pumpkin moon pie?"

Blossom elbows me. "Who cares? It's pumpkin."

I narrow my eyes at her. "You're one of those annoying people who go crazy when pumpkin spice arrives in the grocery store, aren't you?"

She winks. "I'll never tell."

Parker hands us each a pumpkin moon pie. "It's a pumpkin spice cookie filled with marshmallow cream and decorated to resemble the full moon over the tide."

I take a bite and moan as the flavors of pumpkin and marshmallow hit my tongue. "I don't understand how you're not working at some fancy patisserie in a big city somewhere, but Smuggler's Hideaway is lucky to have you."

Pain flashes in her eyes but then she blinks and it's gone. Before I have a chance to ask her what's wrong, a man leans over me.

"My treat," Rhett says as he hands her cash.

"We can pay for ourselves."

"Speak for yourself," Blossom whisper-shouts. "I personally never say no when a gentleman wants to buy me a slice of heaven."

If she only knew. This pumpkin treat is not a slice of heaven. Heaven is spending the night twisted up in the sheets with Rhett. Heaven is him touching and tasting every inch of your body. Heaven is him bringing you wave of pleasure after wave of pleasure.

I wrangle my hormones under control. Rhett may want a relationship but I'm not convinced. My past says men are liars. Even if there are a few good men, I wouldn't be the one to stumble upon one, considering my track record with the opposite sex.

"What are you doing here?" I ask.

He grins. "Where else would I be but with you, Havoc?"

"Sorry, but I'm spending the day with my friend, Blossom."

Blossom raises her hands. "Don't look at me. I'm happy to have the help of a local for *The Smuggler's Gauntlet.*"

"Excellent." Rhett rubs his hands together. "I've played a Prohibition officer for years. We'll have an advantage."

Prohibition officer? "Hold on. What is *The Smuggler's Gauntlet?*"

"It's a contest where you sneak 'contraband' past Prohibition officers. You evade capture in a maze of hidden tunnels, foggy alleyways, and secret doors," he explains.

I frown. "I don't think you want me on your team. I'm not very fast."

"Being fast isn't a requirement. Being sneaky is."

"Don't say I didn't warn you." Another gust of wind rolls in off of the ocean and I shiver.

He frowns. "Are you cold?"

"I'm fine."

He studies me and my chattering teeth. "You are cold." He snags my hand and leads me through the market until we reach a clothing stand.

"I don't need another sweatshirt."

"Too bad because I'm buying you one."

I yank my hand away from his. "You're being controlling again."

He sighs before raking a hand through his hair. "I'm sorry. I don't mean to be controlling. I don't want you to be cold. Let me do this for you, please."

"If you don't let him buy you a sweatshirt, I will," Blossom whispers to me.

"Oh, please. You've got your sights set on Jaxon and I know it."

She sniffs and lifts her nose in the air. "Jaxon doesn't know I exist."

Which is painful for her, so I let it go. I'm not teasing her about the man in the presence of his brother.

"This sweatshirt is cute." Rhett holds up a hoodie with a picture of a seal holding a stop sign on it. "Have you met Sammy yet?"

My brow wrinkles. "Sammy?"

"Arms up."

My body automatically responds to the command in his voice despite my mind still fighting the idea of him buying me anything.

"Good girl," he murmurs as he settles the sweatshirt on my body.

"Sammy?" I prompt again because the warmth in Rhett's eyes is doing weird things to me. Such as making me want to give in to him. But I can't. I know better.

"He's a seal," Rhett explains as he pays for the sweatshirt. "He enjoys lazing in the middle of the street and barking at tourists for attention."

He sounds adorable. "I love seals. I want to meet him."

"We'll go another time. But now we need to kick my brothers' asses at the gauntlet."

"Yes." Blossom pumps her fist.

Rhett takes my hand and steers me through the crowd until we reach the high school. "This is where the gauntlet is held."

Blossom shivers. "A gauntlet in a high school makes total sense."

"It's in the gymnasium," he says as we join the line.

I glance around and notice several people doing stretches. "Remember. I warned you I'm not a runner."

Rhett throws his arm around my shoulders. "They're tourists. Tourists never win the gauntlet."

"Blossom and I aren't native islanders."

He winks. "Good thing you have me."

"How does this work?" Blossom asks.

"We each get a piece of contraband when we enter. The goal is to make it through the gauntlet with the contraband before a Prohibition officer catches you."

"Do the officers have weapons?" Blossom asks.

I gasp. "What?"

She shrugs. "It was only a question. Don't worry. I'm not planning to kick or slap an officer. Unless one happens to be Jaxon."

Rhett barks out a laugh. "Jaxon isn't a guard."

"Bummer," Blossom mutters.

"You ready?" Rhett asks when the door opens in front of us to allow us entrance.

"Does it matter if I say no?" I ask.

Blossom giggles, and Rhett shakes his head.

"I guess I'm ready then."

Blossom rushes inside. I follow her. I feel bad. She really wants to win, but she's stuck with me. Rhett forces his way in front of us so he can pay.

"I can pay for myself," I grumble.

"Speak for yourself," Blossom says.

Once Rhett has paid, the attendant hands us empty whiskey bottles. "This is your contraband. If the bottle breaks before you finish the gauntlet, you'll be disqualified."

He motions us forward. "Wait at the start line. Your time starts when the door opens."

Blossom skips ahead. She shoves the bottle up her sleeve. Rhett puts his bottle in his jeans pocket. I put my bottle in my bra. Rhett's eyes widen.

"What? These big breasts should be good for something."

His eyes flare. "Don't you worry, Havoc. Those breasts of yours are definitely good."

Warmth gathers in my belly at the passion in his blue eyes. Before I have a chance to dim it, the door opens and Blossom dashes inside. "Come on. We're winning this."

Rhett grasps my hand and drags me forward. I'm glad he's leading because I can barely see a foot in front of me with all the fog in the air.

"Stop! Smugglers!" a man shouts from somewhere to my side.

"You can't catch me," Blossom squeals.

"To the left," Rhett coaches her. She goes right and he sighs. "Your other left."

She spins around and nearly crashes into us. He nudges her forward. "This way."

We run through the maze behind Blossom until she leads us to a dead end. Her hands move over the walls. "There must be a hidden passage here somewhere."

There's a click and a door opens. "Found it," Rhett says. Blossom rushes through the door. Rhett goes next. I take up the rear.

The door begins to close and I hurry to get through it, but it closes before I can make it and I crash into it.

The next thing I know, I'm laying on the grass outside the high school with Rhett and Blossom looming over me. "Did we win?"

Rhett grins down at me. "We did."

"Big man carried you the entire way through the gauntlet after you passed out."

I groan. "It wasn't my fault."

Rhett chuckles. "Of course not. The door came out of nowhere and slapped you in the face."

I try to sit up but dizziness hits me and I fall back down.

"Are you okay?" Rhett asks as he brushes the hair from my face.

The concern in his eyes causes a crack in my resistance to form. I need to get out of here and superglue that crack. I can't afford to let my resistance crumble.

Chapter 19

"I'm not thanking my brothers because they accidentally helped." ~ Rhett

RHETT

I stroll into the offices of the distillery and grin at Dakota sitting behind her desk. "Good morning, Havoc."

She glances at the clock before lifting her eyebrows at me. I chuckle.

"I had a meeting with our accountant this morning," I explain as I set a coffee and muffin down on her desk. "Parker claims double espresso is your drink of choice. I figured you'd want one of those girly drinks with more syrup than coffee."

"Syrup doesn't have caffeine in it," she mutters before sipping on her coffee.

She moans and my cock twitches. It remembers every moan and sigh and gasp she made the night we were together. I've played them over and over in my mind. Usually while in the shower with my cock in my hand.

I inhale a deep breath and tell my cock to calm the hell down before I drag Dakota into my office and have my wicked way with her. But I can't. She's still hesitant to date me. I need to wear her down. And I will.

"The muffin is baked peaches and cream whiskey. Parker uses our whiskey in the batter."

"You had me at muffin," she says before stuffing the baked goodie into her mouth.

She licks her bottom lip and I groan. "Stop teasing me, Havoc."

She blinks up at me. "Teasing you? I'm merely sitting at my desk at work, enjoying a muffin. How am I teasing you?"

I narrow my eyes on her. "Act innocent all you want. I know the truth."

She bats her eyelashes. "I have no idea what you mean."

I fist my hands before I haul her out of her chair and show her exactly what I mean.

"And you wonder why I nicknamed you Havoc."

She giggles. The sound is warm and carefree. I'll put up with a lot of blue balls to hear it. Dakota carries the weight of the world on her shoulders. I could help, but the stubborn woman refuses to allow me to. The same way, she refuses to acknowledge there's something special between us.

I will change her mind, but I need to be patient. A trait I'm not exactly known for.

"I want to know why you call her Havoc," Zane says as he saunters into the reception area.

Miles raises his hand as he joins us. "Me too."

"None of your business. Get back to work."

Zane looks at Miles. "Isn't he cute? Thinking he can order us around."

Miles shakes his head. "I prefer the word delusional."

Dakota laughs. "Delusional fits."

I wag my finger at her. "Don't encourage these yahoos."

"Why not?" Zane asks.

"Yea." Miles nods. "Why not?"

"Seriously. Do you want me to tell her about the time I caught the two of you throwing stink bombs into the teachers' lounge in high school?"

"It was a misunderstanding," Miles says. "I never should have been given detention."

I raise an eyebrow. "No? Mouthing off to a teacher isn't cause for detention anymore?"

His nose wrinkles. "Define mouthing off."

"Telling the teacher she doesn't know what the hell she's talking about."

A muscle twitches in his jaw. "She was the guidance counselor and told me I'd never be a professional surfer."

Damn. Miles's past as a surfer is a sore subject. He tore his rotator cuff at a competition in Hawaii and hasn't been the same since. All the physical therapy in the world wasn't enough to give him the range of motion he needs to surf professionally.

Zane throws an arm over Miles's shoulders. "She definitely didn't know what she was talking about."

Miles shrugs Zane off. He doesn't want pity. Too bad he doesn't understand there's a difference between pity and compassion.

"I've never surfed before," Dakota says, and I could kiss her for cutting the tension in the room.

Miles gasps. "You've never surfed before?"

She shrugs. "I've never even swam in the ocean."

Miles leans against her desk in front of her. "You've never swam in the ocean?" She shakes her head. "But you can swim, can't you?"

Her nose wrinkles. "I know how to doggy paddle."

He grasps her hand. "I'll teach you how to swim."

I wrench him away from Dakota. "Don't touch her."

"Uh oh. Mr. Overprotector has arrived at the party." Miles barks out a laugh at his own joke. He's not funny.

I glare at him. "She didn't give you permission to touch her. You don't touch a woman without her permission. I know I taught you this."

"Dakota doesn't mind," Miles claims. "We're buds. Aren't we?"

I stand in front of Dakota and block her from his view. "Being work colleagues doesn't mean you're buds, and it doesn't give you permission to touch someone."

He waggles his eyebrows. "She can touch me if she wants. We'll call it even."

"You're not listening to me."

"Because you're being boring," Zane says.

I cross my arms over my chest and stare my two brothers down. "It's boring to discuss how to treat a lady? Should I tell Mom this is how you feel?"

Zane groans. "You're such a tattletale."

"Here are words I never thought I'd say. Let's go back to work." Miles starts toward his office.

"But we never did figure out why Rhett calls Dakota Havoc," Zane says as he follows him down the hallway.

I wait a few seconds after they disappear. It wouldn't be the first time they faked leaving to eavesdrop on a conversation. But they don't make a reappearance.

"I apologize for their behavior. I'll speak to them again about touching you without your permission."

"Thank you." Dakota's face goes all soft, and my hackles rise.

"Did…" I swallow the lump in my throat and force the question out of my mouth. "Was your husband ever physically violent with you?"

"No." She shakes her head. "I thought we were in love until the day he died."

I scowl. I don't want her thinking about being in love with her dead husband. I want her fixated on me the way I am on her.

She scoffs. "I didn't realize I'd fallen out of love with him long before his death."

I frown. How do you not realize you've fallen out of love with someone? I nearly open my mouth to ask, when I remember we're in the office, where my brothers could still be eavesdropping. This isn't a conversation for now. This is a conversation for a date. Speaking of which.

"Do you want to go out on a date with me?" I babble on before she has a chance to reject me. "I had a good time at the

Ghost Tide Festival. I'm good at winning, but I'm also handy for when doors come up and bite you. And I can—"

"Yes."

"And also…" I trail off when I realize what she said. "Yes?"

She nods, but her smile is shaky and unsure. Did I push her too far?

I start to backpedal. I don't want her to feel obligated to go out on a date with me. I want her excited to spend time with me, the way I am with her. "We don't have to…"

Zane and Miles rush into the room singing, "Dakota and Rhett sitting in a tree. K-i-s-s-i-n-g."

Dakota's cheeks darken until they're the color of the ocean when the algae blooms. I growl. "You will not embarrass Dakota."

They skip to a stop, and Zane rolls his eyes. "We're only having fun."

"You can have fun without embarrassing her. Do you hear me?"

Zane salutes. "Loud and clear."

I stare at Miles until he sighs. "I hear you, Mr. Boring."

"Good. Now, apologize to Dakota for embarrassing her."

"We're sorry, Dakota," they say in unison.

"It's okay," she whispers.

Zane saunters toward her. "If you ever get tired of bossy-pants, I can—"

I prowl toward him. Miles shackles Zane's wrist and hauls him away. "Come on. I think they want to be alone."

I start after them. I taught them better than this. They should know how to behave in front of a woman.

"Thanks for proving me right," Dakota says, and I stop.

"Proving you right?"

"To give you a chance."

I smirk. "Get used to it, Havoc. I'm right a lot."

She giggles and I realize I'd throw my brothers off a cliff to hear the sound of her happiness. "It's funny you think so, Mr. High and Mighty."

"Mr. High and Mighty? I'll show you High and Mighty." I wiggle my hands as I approach her.

"No tickling," she screeches.

I drop my hands. "You're lucky I'm a gentleman. Most of the time." I wink and her green eyes flare with passion.

I can't wait to have Dakota naked in my bed again, but I know better than to pressure her. Getting her to agree to a date was hard enough. I need to take it slow. Get her used to me being in her life. Get her addicted to me.

And then, I'll show her I'm not the least bit boring.

Chapter 20

"Rhett is a dark horse and I'm finding the idea of horseback riding more and more appealing." ~ Dakota

DAKOTA

This is stupid. This is a mistake. I dig my phone out of my jeans pocket – intent on messaging Rhett to say I changed my mind – but my finger hesitates over the send button. I made an agreement. I need to stick to it.

"You're going to wear a hole in the carpet," Sadie says.

I stop pacing to point to the floor. "Really? You're worried about this carpet?"

She wags her finger at me. "Nope. We're not discussing the carpet."

I give her my back to stare out of the window. I have a sneaking suspicion I know what she wants to discuss and I'm not interested.

"You're going to ignore me when I know you can hear me?"

"Yep."

She giggles. "This is fun. Way more fun than when my sister, Scarlett, fell in love with Weston."

She told me all about how her older sister ended up trapped in a log cabin with a police officer during a snowstorm this past Christmas. Scarlett hated Weston because he teased her in high school, but somehow, they fell in love during the time they spent together.

"This is not a love story."

"Did you tell Rhett it's not a love story?"

I told him entirely too much about my past. I thought he'd run in the other direction. Instead, he offered to pay off my debts – no, thank you, I don't need a man to save me – and asked me out.

I tried to resist him. I truly did. But when he yelled at his brothers in defense of me, I caved. The crack in my walls blew wide open and I said yes before I had the chance to grab some mortar and fix my fortifications.

"I'll answer your question if you tell me why you race to the mailbox whenever the mail is delivered."

She frowns. I knew she wouldn't answer my question. When she gets a letter, she rushes to the restroom and locks the door behind her to read it.

"Where are you going?" she asks instead.

All my anxiety comes rushing back, and I wring my hands together. "I don't know."

All I know is he said to dress casually and not to bring a purse. My mind is whirling with possibilities. Or, rather, the lack of possibilities. What do you do on a date in jeans? How come I'm not allowed to bring my purse?

Rhett's SUV turns into the parking lot of the *Mermaid Motel* and I hurry toward the entrance.

Sadie whistles. "That is some vehicle."

"What do you mean? It's an SUV. There are tons of them on the island."

She snorts. "But very few of them cost as much as most people earn in a year."

Great. Something else to worry about. Rhett is wealthy. How could I have forgotten? My boss is a billionaire and they're brothers.

"Have fun!" Sadie hollers as I rush outside.

Rhett frowns as he walks toward me. "I wanted to be a gentleman and pick you up at your door."

"I'll let you open the car door," I offer.

"You drive a hard bargain, Havoc." He opens the door, but when I try to climb inside the vehicle, he grasps my hips and helps me up. Then, he leans over me to fasten my seatbelt.

"I could have climbed inside on my own."

He tweaks my nose. "But now you didn't need to."

He shuts the door before I have a chance to respond.

"Where are we going?" I ask the second he opens his door.

He chuckles. "Impatient?"

"Curious."

"What I say next has to remain strictly confidential between the two of us."

I groan. "I am not robbing a bank with you. You do realize banks don't actually have cash anymore?"

"I won't rob a bank unless I have to."

"I'm confused. Why would you have to rob a bank?"

He switches on the engine and drives away from the motel. "You've met my brothers."

"I never realized siblings could be close but drive each other batty at the same time."

He reaches across the console to squeeze my hand. "I'm sorry you grew up without siblings."

"Judging by the way you are with your siblings, I'd have more scars if I did."

"Don't do that."

"Do what? Make fun of your family? I'm sorry."

"You can make fun of my brothers all you want. Have at it. What I meant is, don't be flippant about how you grew up. You're allowed to be sad for missing out."

I glance out the window. "I never thought of it as missing out."

"Can I ask how you ended up in care?"

I debate what I should say. Before I come up with an answer, he sighs. "I'm sorry. You don't have to answer me if it's painful. Pick another topic."

"It's not painful. I just never discuss this stuff."

"I get it. It's private. You're a very private person."

Am I? I've never had the time or energy to self reflect or go to therapy. I was too busy going to school and working, and then working and building a life, and now trying to survive. Therapy is for people who can afford it.[1]

"My mother was an addict. I was born addicted to heroin. While I was in the NICU, my mother left the hospital and was never seen again. She was admitted under a false name. I never knew her real name or who my dad was."

"Shit, Dakota. I'm sorry."

"Why are you sorry? You had nothing to do with it."

He sighs. "You know what I mean. I'm sorry for all you went through."

I shrug. "I don't remember it."

"And no one ever wanted to adopt you?"

"Children born addicted have a higher risk of developing long-term problems. No one wanted to accept the risk." It's true. Just not the entire truth.

"Assholes."

My brow wrinkles. "They're not assholes. Having a sick child can be costly."

"It doesn't matter. When you love your children, you do everything for them."

"You make it sound easy."

He chuckles. "It's not easy. It's hard as shit. When Dad left us, I wasn't even fifteen. Eli was older, but Jaxon, Miles, Zane, and Kai were all younger. Eli and I worked our asses off to

---

1. Please don't tell my therapist I wrote that. She'd have a field day.

make sure our four brothers had everything they ever wanted or needed."

"What about your mom? Where was she?"

"In between working two jobs, she was falling apart because the man she'd loved her whole life left her for another woman."

My heart aches for her. I know how she felt.

Rhett squeezes my hand. "Enough about them. I want us to have fun today."

"And how are we going to have fun?"

He nods toward the road sign. "Guess."

"This is Pirate's Perch?" I ask as I glance around. There isn't much to see. A few houses along the main drag, but there aren't any stores of any kind.

"It's the smallest town on Smuggler's Hideaway."

"This is not a town. Maybe a hamlet?"

"It is pretty small. Almost all of the shops on the island are located in Smuggler's Rest."

"What are we doing here?"

"Can you guess?"

"Can I get a clue? Because the only thing I can imagine doing here is sitting on a porch in a rocking chair watching paint dry."

"I'll give you a clue. Viking."

Viking? What does he mean? Are we searching for a Scandinavian seafaring pirate? History wasn't my subject, but I'm pretty sure the Vikings restricted their raiding to north-western Europe.

I gasp when I realize where I've heard the word Viking recently. "Did the otter escape? Shouldn't we organize a search party? The two of us alone will never find her."

"Viking is perfectly safe. She's in Smuggler's Rest, where she belongs. Not in Pirate's Perch, where another animal belongs."

"I know each town has a live mascot, but I don't remember what the Pirate's Perch mascot is."

"It's a parrot named Plank."

My mouth drops open when I remember another tidbit about the live mascots. "Are we going to steal him?"

Rhett smirks. "We are. And then we're going to rub it in my brothers' noses."

"Do you know where Plank is?"

"I happen to know who is hiding Plank and this person happens to be working overtime today."

I bounce in my seat. "This is exciting. I've never seen a parrot up close before. Do they really talk? Are they mean? Will he poop on us? Should we have a cage for him?"

Rhett laughs and points to the backseat. "I've got a cage but I make no guarantees he won't poop on us. Plank is a foul-mouthed asshole."

"You've tried to steal him before, haven't you?"

"Back in high school. Jaxon and I teamed up. It was not the best team. Jaxon kept reading instructions from his phone but he refused to help otherwise."

I rub my hands together. "Don't you worry. I'll help."

"Do you love all animals or just otters and parrots?"

"I love them all. Animals are sweet and cuddly. Humans not so much."

"I don't guarantee Plank will be sweet and cuddly."

He turns down a driveway and we bump around as he drives the unpaved road for a few minutes until we arrive at a cabin in the woods.

"Phew," I say when the cabin appears. "I was worried you were leading me into the woods for nefarious reasons."

He switches off the engine and glances over at me. His blue eyes are full of heat, and I shiver at the promise in them. "Whenever you want me to kidnap you for nefarious reasons, you let me know. I'll get the handcuffs ready."

My jaw drops open. I've never used handcuffs in the bedroom before. But judging by the tingling in my nether regions, I'm ready to try. With Rhett. No one else.

He pinches my jaw and shuts my mouth. "You're trouble, Havoc."

He kisses my nose before jumping out of the vehicle. He rounds the front and I wait for him. I might as well enjoy his gentlemanly act for as long as it lasts.

He opens the door and grasps my hips. His fingers dig in as he lifts me to set me on the ground. I remember how good those fingertips felt digging into my hips as he sank into me from behind.

"Trouble," he murmurs before pressing his lips against mine in an all too brief kiss.

"Says the man who wants to commit a felony on our first date."

He chuckles as he takes my hand and leads me around the cabin to the shed out back.

I frown. "Is Plank in the shed?"

"Nope. But the extra key to the back door is."

I wait by the back door as Rhett sneaks across the yard to the shed. He opens the door – it's unlocked – and snatches a set of keys from inside.

"Is there anyone home?" he asks as he returns to me.

Damn. Was I supposed to be doing reconnaissance? I suck at committing felonies. I blame Rhett's ass. It's very distracting. And sexy.

"I don't think so," I hedge.

We listen at the door for a minute but when we don't hear any movement inside, Rhett unlocks the door and we tiptoe into the house.

"Where's Plank?" I whisper as we walk through the kitchen.

"Where's Plank? Where's Plank?" A not quite human voice mimics.

"I think we found him." Rhett points to the bird in the cage in the corner of the living room.

"He's pretty," I say as I walk toward him. He's a vibrant red with blue and yellow on his wings.

"Plank's pretty," the bird mimics.

"And you're smart, too."

"Pretty and smart," it mimics again.

"You can continue to flirt with the bird on the way back to Smuggler's Rest," Rhett says. "We shouldn't stay too long. We don't want to be caught."

"Because we're committing a felony."

Rhett opens the door to the cage and reaches for the bird. It pecks at him and he snatches his hand back. "Ouch."

"I want the sexy one," the bird says.

I giggle. "I didn't realize parrots talked this much."

"Stop flirting with my girlfriend," Rhett grumbles at the bird.

"She's out of your league," it says.

I clap a hand over my mouth before I laugh out loud. "I love you, Plank."

"Plank loves you, too."

"Shall I get him?" I ask Rhett.

"Crap. I forgot the cage."

"Crap. I forgot the cage," the bird mimics.

I study the parrot. He appears gentle, but I've never handled a bird before. I'm a bit apprehensive about stealing him from his cage. What if he flies away? He's domesticated. He'll never survive in the wild.

"Freeze! Hands up!"

I scream and rush for the door. I am not getting arrested for stealing a parrot. Rhett chases after me.

"Stop, Havoc, it was Plank. He was pretending to be a cop."

I screech to a halt on the back porch. I grab my side where I can feel a stitch forming. I wasn't kidding about not being a runner.

"Okay," I gasp out. "Get the cage and we'll go back."

He heads for his vehicle but swears and pivots on his heel to return to me. "There's a car coming. We need to get out of here."

He shackles my wrist and leads me around the house. We jump into his SUV and he drives away as fast as possible on the bumpy driveway. We pass a car and I wave to the occupant, who wags his finger at me.

"Close call," Rhett says as we turn onto the main road.

"But it was fun. Especially since Plank liked me more than you."

"Of course, he did. You're magnificent."

I wait for the punchline, but apparently there isn't one. He's serious. He thinks I'm magnificent. No wonder I'm falling in love with him.

My world tilts and I grab the door handle before I fall over. Falling in love with Rhett? I can't fall in love with anyone. I should know better.

Apparently, my heart doesn't care. It wants what it wants.

Chapter 21

"Great. This bird does like me." ~ Rhett

RHETT

"Where are we going?" Dakota asks as we drive away from the *Mermaid Motel*, where I picked her up from the reception area. She grimaces as we travel over a bump in the parking lot and her cheeks pinken.

I frown. Is she ashamed of living at the motel? There's no reason for her to feel ashamed. She's working her ass off to pay the debts of her late husband. Debts she shouldn't have to pay. Debts she won't let me pay.

"Uh oh. You don't appear happy. What's wrong? Are we going to commit another felony? Are you worried all the animals will like me better than you?"

I reach across the console to place my hand on her thigh. I can't stop touching her when she's near. Even if I'm trying to hold off sex until she's convinced I'm serious about this relationship.

I never thought I'd be serious about a woman. Not after watching my dad tell Mom he loved her before driving away to his new life with a different woman. I never thought I'd be able to trust a woman enough to be in a serious relationship. But Dakota bared her soul to me. And I can't resist her.

"I'm certain all animals will like you more than me."

She grins at me. "Of course, they will. I'm sweet, not sour the way you are."

I play growl at her. "You think I'm sour."

She shrugs. "They don't call you Mr. High and Mighty for nothing."

"They?" I raise a brow. "You're the one who coined the phrase."

"For a reason," she sings.

"And now my brothers think it's cute to use the nickname."

She pats my hand. "Poor baby. Can't handle a bit of teasing from his brothers."

I clear my throat. "Speaking of brothers…"

"Uh oh. What did they do now? Do we need to bail them out? Is there a jail on Smuggler's Hideaway?"

"There is a jail on the island. It's actually quite nice."

"How do you know?" She holds up a hand. "On second thought, don't tell me."

I chuckle. "It wasn't my fault."

"Of course not."

"Anyway, my brothers."

"Yes…"

"They're joining us today."

Her brow wrinkles. "Your brothers are joining us? If this is some kind of weird reverse harem thing, count me out. I have my hands full with one Raider. I don't need more."

I smirk. "You have your hands full with one Raider?"

Her cheeks darken. "You know what I mean."

"No, I don't. Explain."

She slaps my shoulder. "Don't embarrass me."

I immediately sober. "Sorry. I would never embarrass you on purpose."

She blows out a breath. "You're more of a gentleman than I deserve."

"Wrong, Havoc. You deserve everything."

I turn into the parking lot of *Barnacles & Barnyards,* the petting zoo on the island, and find a spot to park.

"Today is Kai's birthday. Since he lost at poker, he has to go to the petting zoo for his birthday."

Her mouth drops open and panic fills her eyes. "It's Kai's birthday? How do I not know this? I didn't buy him a present."

I squeeze her hand. "I put your name on our present."

"I hope it wasn't lame."

"Tickets to a comedy show on the mainland."

She nods. "Good idea."

"But," I prod when it's obvious she wants to say more.

"What am I doing here?" she bursts out. "I'm not part of the family. Yes, I work for your brother. And I work with the family. But it's work."

My growl isn't playful anymore. "You're my girlfriend." She opens her mouth to protest and I amend myself. "The woman I'm dating."

And I want to show her how it feels to be part of a family. I want to give her a family because I'm falling in love with her.

The revelation doesn't surprise me. It probably should, considering how much she annoyed me when we first met. But I'm coming to understand the annoyance was fear upon recognizing my other half.

Dakota squirms in her seat. "I don't know about this."

"I understand you're nervous, but you know almost everyone here. My brothers, Eli's girlfriend Paisley."

Eli and Paisley are no longer just fooling around behind closed doors at the distillery. They're a solid couple who are very much in love. I couldn't be happier for him. Although I still give him shit. It's my obligation as his brother.

"Almost isn't very reassuring."

I chuckle. "Don't worry. I'll protect you."

She squares her shoulders. "I don't need protecting."

"There's my girl," I mutter before kissing her nose. "Let me open your door."

I jump out of my SUV. I wave to my family as they walk toward us. I round the vehicle to open Dakota's door, but Miles arrives and opens it for her before I get there.

"Milady." He tries to bow but I shove him.

"Leave her alone."

"Mom!" Miles shouts. "Rhett won't share his toys."

I squeeze his neck and slam him against the SUV. "Dakota is not a toy."

He holds up his hands. "Just testing."

"I'll test you," I grumble.

"I have ten dollars on Miles," Zane says.

"Twenty on Rhett," Dakota counters.

"I'm with Dakota," Paisley adds.

"Boys," Mom chides and I release Miles. I find Dakota and wrap an arm around her.

Mom beams at me. "Is this Dakota? It's lovely to meet you."

I keep my arm tight around Dakota. If Mom hugs her and welcomes her to the family, she'll flee before I have a chance to explain to Mom what's happening.

"Dakota, this is my mom and her husband, Stuart," I introduce.

Dakota smiles at them. "It's lovely to meet you both."

"The introductions are done," Kai declares. "Let's go enjoy my birthday!"

"At a petting zoo," Dakota mutters.

Paisley giggles. "You should have been there for the last birthday. We went to *Mermaid Mystical Gardens.* It was a blast."

Eli snorts. "We got kicked out."

Paisley purses her lips. "We did not get kicked out."

"They asked us to vacate the premises."

"But they couldn't catch us to kick us out."

Dakota giggles. "And here I thought you were some brainiac."

"Nah." Paisley shakes her head. "Jaxon's the brainiac. I'm the chemistry nerd."

"I'll amend the distillery meeting notes to reflect the proper names," Dakota sasses and I grin. She's going to fit in with this group of misfits just fine.

"Come on." Kai motions to us from the entrance, where he's already waiting.

"I've plotted out a route," he says when we reach him. "We'll begin with Captain Cluck. Then, it's off to visit Rumrunner the mischievous goat, Bootlegger the miniature donkey, Old Salty the llama, the mer-cows and the mer-pigs, and we'll finish at the tortoise race."

"What are mer-cows and mer-pigs?" Dakota asks.

"Mer-cows are cows that swam to shore from a shipwreck," Kai explains. "And Mer-goats resemble mermaids with their unusually long, silky coats."

"I brought my flask." Paisley offers it to Dakota, who holds up her hand.

"I'm not much of a drinker."

Zane sighs. "And here I thought you were cool."

"Unlike you, I don't need to drink to be cool."

I chuckle, and Zane glares at me. "He doesn't drink much either. You two are meant for each other."

Yes, we are. But not because of some bullshit about not drinking.

Once the others finish sipping from the flask, we begin walking through the petting zoo. I hold Dakota's hand as we stroll. I was never much for holding a girl's hand but Dakota's different. Touching her is an addiction I have no desire to cure myself of.

"Ta da!" Kai motions to a chicken. "Meet the seafaring chicken, Captain Cluck."

"Seafaring?" Dakota asks.

Before anyone can answer, the chicken clucks and flies up to land on my shoulder. I try to shove him off, but he digs his claws in. "Go away, Captain Cluck."

Dakota bursts into laughter. "And here I thought all birds hated you."

I glare at her. "Plank is an asshole."

My words cause her to double over in laughter. "Only Mr. High and Mighty would say a parrot is an asshole."

"Can someone get this bird off of me?" I ask my family.

Eli taps his chin as he studies me. "I bet he can't keep Captain Cluck on his shoulder for five minutes without losing his control."

Zane rolls his eyes. "This is Mr. Control. He'll make it thirty minutes."

I glare at my brothers. "You're all assholes." I turn to Dakota. "You're the bird whisperer. Can you help me?"

She raises her palms. "I don't want to cheat. Bets have been placed."

"You didn't place one, so what does it matter?"

Her eyes spark with challenge. "How about this? If you manage to keep Captain Cluck on your shoulder all day, I'll go out on another date with you."

Kai rubs his hands together. "This is going to be fun. Jaxon, research how to bribe a chicken."

Jaxon digs his phone out and I snarl at him. "What are you doing?"

He pushes his glasses up his nose. "I believe you would term this 'having fun'."

"Children," Mom begins but Stuart cuts her off.

"Let them have their fun. They're not hurting anyone."

Mom sighs – the signal she's giving in – and Stuart kisses her hair.

I mock glare at him. "And here I defended you when my asshole brothers wanted to prank you to force you to leave Mom."

"They did prank me. Multiple times."

"Does anyone have any snacks?" Jaxon asks.

Dakota opens her bag and digs around. "I have peanut butter crackers."

I shackle her wrist to stop her. "Do you not want to go out on another date with me?"

She looks up at me from beneath her lashes. "Maybe I think you should earn it."

I straighten my shoulders. "I'll earn it." I try petting the chicken. "Good little Captain Cluck."

Apparently, chickens don't enjoy being petted because he clucks and flaps his wings. I turn my head before I end up with a black eye from a chicken.

"Here you go, Captain Cluck." Dakota offers him a bit of cracker and he eats from her hand. She continues to feed him until the cracker is gone.

"Do all animals love you?"

"Not dead snakes." She shivers.

Damn. I didn't mean to bring up the loan shark who's bothering her. If I had more than a first name, I'd pay off those debts. To hell with what Dakota wants. I won't allow her to be in danger.

"Here, Captain Cluck. Here. Here," Miles calls. If a chicken could snub its nose, I'd say that was Captain Cluck's response.

"I've got a better idea." Zane tiptoes behind me. I try to spin around – I know better than to let a brother sneak up behind me – but Kai grasps my hips to stop me.

"BOO!" Zane shouts.

Captain Cluck clucks and flaps his wings. His claws dig into my shoulder as he jumps off.

"You cheated," I grumble at Zane.

"Someone's not getting another date with Dakota," Miles sings.

"Oh no, you're bleeding." Dakota pulls the neckline of my t-shirt to the side to reveal two lines of blood.

"There's a first aid kit near the goat enclosure." Paisley points to it. "And don't ask me how I know."

Dakota shackles my wrist and drags me away.

"I'm okay, Havoc. It's only a little bit of blood."

"I know, but I don't want to be near your brothers when I tell you you're getting another date even though you lost the bet."

I tug on her hand to stop her. "I'm getting another date?"

"You allowed a chicken to maul you. I think you deserve another date."

I wiggle my eyebrows. "What about a kiss? Do I deserve one of those?"

She sighs. "If you must."

I don't need to ask twice. I haul her near and meld my lips to hers. Her taste of strawberry and sin hits me and I groan. I'll let a chicken maul me any day if this is my reward. I'm afraid there's not much I wouldn't do to have the privilege of touching Dakota.

I'm falling for this woman and there's no way I can stop it.

It's possible I don't want to.

Chapter 22

"Never accept love advice from a seal that thinks it's a stop sign." ~ Dakota

DAKOTA

I smile at Rhett when I open my door. Yep, my door. I allowed him to meet me at my door instead of running out of the reception like a sixteen-year-old on my first date.

Of course, I also allowed him to drop me off here. And kiss me until I couldn't breathe. But I didn't invite him in. My heart is falling for this man, but I still control my body – barely – and I'm being cautious.

"You ready for our date?"

I lift my bag, packed with a towel and dry clothes. "At least this time you told me where we're going."

He smirks. "Did I?"

"Yes. We're going swimming."

"But where?"

"At the community pool." Where else would we go?

"You'll see."

He snatches the bag from me before offering me his elbow. I thread my arm through his and he leads me to his vehicle.

"Are we not going to the community pool?" I ask once we're driving.

"There is no community pool."

My nose wrinkles. "There's no swimming pool on Smuggler's Hideaway?"

"Not what I said. I said there's no community pool."

I cross my arms over my chest. "I don't like it when you're being mysterious."

"Yes, you do." He winks at me. "Our first stop isn't the pool."

"It isn't?"

He hands me his phone. "Open the Sammy app?"

"Sammy app?"

"It's an app to figure out where Sammy the seal is."

"Sammy the seal!" I squeal. "I'm dying to meet him."

"I know." He taps his phone. "Find out where he is on the app."

"Your phone's locked." I try handing it back to him.

"My passcode is 524524."

My jaw drops. "You just gave me your passcode."

"I'm aware since I did it."

"But I could go into your phone and read your messages or your emails. I could get onto your social media and tell the world you identify as a purple monster."

He chuckles. "A purple monster? I couldn't be a normal monster?"

I slap his arm. "Don't make fun of me."

He pulls to the side of the road and puts the vehicle in park. "Dakota." He palms my neck to bring me near. "If I'm with someone, I have to trust them one hundred percent. Which means giving her access to my phone and my life."

"You trust me one hundred percent?"

"I do."

Guilt rears its ugly head. Rhett doesn't know all of my secrets. I didn't tell him every last one because I'm afraid he'd run if he knew everything about me.

"But you barely know me," I argue, since – despite the guilt clamoring around in my chest – I'm not ready to confess all to him.

"I know you're gorgeous and wicked smart and full of optimism despite all the shit life has thrown at you. I know you're loyal. I know enough."

Tears well in my eyes. He didn't say he loves me but his words mean more. Rhett sees me. The real me.

"Thank you."

He kisses my forehead before releasing me and putting the SUV in gear. "Now, open the Sammy app and tell me where to drive."

I suck up my tears and concentrate on the task at hand. The app is easy enough to find. The icon is of a seal holding a stop sign.

"He was last spotted on the road leading to the *Hideaway Haven Resort*."

"He'll probably still be in the area then. Sammy's a bit lazy."

Excitement buzzes through me as we drive toward the resort. Luckily, it isn't far as the anticipation is killing me. Rhett slows down as we near the location where the seal was last spotted.

I notice a lump in the middle of the road. "Stop! Stop! It's him."

Rhett pulls to the side of the road and switches on his emergency lights. This time, I don't wait for him to open my door. I rush out and hurry toward the gray lump in the middle of the street.

"Sammy!"

He barks in response and I kneel in front of him.

"I'm Dakota. It's nice to meet you."

He barks again.

Rhett kneels next to me. "Don't get too close to him. He's still a wild animal."

"I know. I've been researching seals ever since you told me about Sammy."

Sammy barks.

"Sorry, Sammy boy. I didn't mean to ignore you."

He makes a chirping noise.

"I think he likes me."

"Of course, he does. All the animals adore you."

I grin up at him. "I am pretty adorable."

His gaze drops to my mouth. "Yes, you are."

His head descends toward mine but before our lips can meet, Sammy growls. I giggle. "I don't think Sammy approves of us kissing."

"Sammy," Rhett grumbles. "You can't steal Dakota away from me."

Sammy whistles.

"You are the funniest seal I've ever met. Although, I've never actually met another seal. My high school class went to an aquarium once, but I didn't get to go since my foster parents couldn't afford to pay the twenty-five-dollar entry."

"I'll take you to an aquarium. There's a nice one about an hour away."

I pat Rhett's thigh. "It's not your job to make up for all the things I missed growing up."

"Don't care. I'm taking on the job whether you want me to or not."

"Did you hear, Sammy? Mr. High and Mighty thinks he's my protector." I lean close to whisper to him. "He's also controlling."

Sammy whistles again.

"I don't approve of controlling men either," I tell him.

Rhett squeezes my hand. "I'm trying not to be controlling."

"He needs to try harder," I tell Sammy.

"Was your late husband controlling?"

I wait for Sammy to interrupt but he appears as curious as Rhett. Darn it. I hate admitting what a fool I was. But this is Rhett – the man I'm falling for – and I'm keeping enough secrets from him.

I blow out a breath and admit the truth. "My dead husband controlled our finances. Whenever I asked questions, he told me not to worry." And there was a lot to worry about.

"I'm sorry. I promise to try harder."

"Thank you. And thank you for not pointing out what a fool I was."

"You weren't a fool. You were…Crap," Rhett swears before jumping to his feet.

"What? What's wrong?"

He points to a car speeding down the road. It's aiming straight for us. My heart lodges in my throat. Oh no. They're going to hit Sammy. Rhett waves his arms at the car.

I shoo Sammy toward the side of the road. "Move, Sammy boy. This car is going to hit you and make you into seal meat. Which I'm pretty sure is illegal to sell and doesn't taste good anyway."

He trills at me.

"Okay, fine. I admit seal fat is different and could be considered a delicacy. Will you please move now?"

I swear he snorts at me before scooting to the side of the road and disappearing.

Rhett tackles me and we tumble to the ground as the car flies by us.

"It didn't even slow down," I say as I watch its taillights disappear.

Rhett rolls over until he's kneeling above me. "Are you okay? Did you get hurt?"

"Me? Get hurt? You're the one who landed on the bottom of our near miss sandwich."

"Do not joke now. It's not funny. Are you hurt?"

He pats my arms and legs.

"I'm not hurt, but go ahead and pat me down as much as you want. You won't hear me complain."

"You're crazy."

"Not crazy but I do want to point out that I'm not the reason we ended up on the ground this time."

He shakes his head before getting to his feet. He offers me his hand. "Are you ready for the second portion of our date, or do you prefer to relax?"

I brush the dirt from my jeans. "It takes more than an asshole driver to traumatize me. I can't wait to find out what you have planned for the second portion of our date."

He herds me toward his SUV and helps me inside. I push him away. "Stop trying to make sure I'm not injured. I'm fine."

He grunts before rounding the vehicle and climbing into the driver's side.

"Where are we going now?"

"Swimming in the ocean."

Excitement and fear battle for top billing in my emotions. I'm excited to swim in the ocean for the first time, but I'm a bit afraid.

"I'm not the best swimmer."

He squeezes my thigh. "Don't worry, Havoc. I'll be by your side the entire time."

"You won't let me drown?"

"I won't let any harm come to you ever if I can help it."

It's official. Excitement is the winner of the battle for my emotions. You can't help but love a man who claims he'll protect you forever.

Not that I love Rhett. Not yet, at least. I admit I'm falling for him. But love? I'm not certain I know how love feels. I haven't had the best experience in the love and devotion department.

"I can protect you. I was a lifeguard in high school."

"You were a lifeguard in high school?"

He snorts. "I didn't have much choice."

"Let me guess. You were watching out for your brothers."

He sighs. "They're the bane of my existence."

The way he protects his brothers is a thing of beauty. I've never met a man who put protecting others in front of his own pleasure. It's intoxicating.

"Thanks for going swimming with me," I say when he parks in a small lot near the beach.

"You don't need to thank me. You never need to thank me for giving you things you want."

"What if what I want is to thank you?"

"My Havoc," he mutters before kissing my nose. "You're going to be the death of me."

"But what a glorious death it'll be."

"That it will. That it will."

I was joking, but Rhett's voice was dead serious. The things he says has the precarious control I have over my heart wavering. I need to find some mortar and build my walls back up or I won't be able to stop myself from falling head over heels in love with this man.

Chapter 23

"I will not let a swimsuit defeat me." ~ *Rhett*

RHETT

Dakota fiddles with the strap on her bag as she stares up at me. "Do you want to come in?"

I step close until she's pressed against the door to her suite. "Why? Do you want to discuss your swimming technique?"

I don't know if my dick can handle discussing swimming with her. It's about to burst out of my pants as it is after spending the past two hours watching her walk around in a wet, clingy swimsuit.

She bites her lip and I nearly come in my jeans. "Does my swimming technique need improvement?"

"You've got the doggy paddle down." I pinch her chin. "How about I come inside and we have a nightcap?"

Her nose wrinkles. "You don't drink and neither do I."

I caress her cheek. "How about I come inside and we watch some television?"

"I only get two channels and they're both fuzzy."

I lean down to whisper in her ear. "Whatever will we do if I come inside?"

She shivers and I lick the spot behind her ear. "I-I-I don't know."

"I can think of a few ideas." I bite her earlobe and she moans. "Unlock the door, Havoc."

She blinks up at me for a few moments before whirling around to unlock the door. In her haste to get inside, she trips on the sill.

I catch her before she lands face first on the floor. I wrap my arm around her waist from behind while I kick the door shut.

"You okay?"

"Fine. The door hates me."

I chuckle. "Sure. Let's blame it on the door."

She glances at me over her shoulder. "Who else are we going to blame?"

I smirk. "Not you, Havoc. Never you."

Her eyes narrow. "Don't be condescending, Mr. High and Mighty."

I press my hard length into her back and her breath hitches. "I'm not being condescending. I'm moving on to the next portion of our date."

"Did you plan this? Is this some big seduction scene? This is the third date and now it's time for me to put out?"

I let her go before retreating. "I didn't plan this. In fact, I hadn't planned to seduce you again until you …"

I trail off before I can admit the truth. Until she's as addicted to me as I am to her.

"Until I what?"

"Until you're sure of me. Of us. You were hesitant to date me, and I don't want to push you." All true. Not what I was thinking, but still true.

She shakes her head and my cock deflates. It's another cold shower for me tonight.

"You're not pushing me. I was being a brat. Sometimes I'm…" She fiddles with the hem of her t-shirt.

My fingers itch to reach out and touch her. But I shove my hands in my pockets instead. I don't want her to change her mind because her body wants me. I want her to change her mind because *she* wants me.

"What?" I ask.

"Sometimes I'm a bit overwhelmed by you. You're a freaking millionaire."

"I wasn't born a millionaire. I understand struggling for money. I would never judge someone for struggling."

She grunts. "Do you always have to say the perfect thing?"

I smirk. "No."

"And you're you."

"It's true. I am me."

She frowns. "Don't be cute. I mean. You're you." She motions toward my body. "And I'm me." She waves a hand over herself.

I growl. "No one says nasty things about your body. Not even you. Your body is sexy as hell. I've been fighting a hard-on all afternoon."

Her gaze drops to my crotch. "You have?"

"You were in a swimsuit. What did you expect?"

Dakota has no idea how sexy she is. Every man at the beach was mesmerized by her and she didn't notice. It's refreshing being with a woman who has no idea of the power she could wield over men.

But I don't want her to feel self-conscious. I want her to own her body.

I stalk toward her and she retreats until her legs hit the sofa. I wind an arm around her waist before she falls. My Havoc is a klutz, but I don't mind since it gives me the chance to catch her often. And I do enjoy catching her.

"Your swimsuit clung to your every curve. I was worried I'd have to go to the restroom and jack off before I exploded at some point."

"You were?" She bites her bottom lip.

I tug her lip from her teeth. "Only I get to bite you."

"Bite me? You want to bite me?"

I draw a hand up her side to her breast. "Starting here." I move my hand down and around to her ass. "And moving on to here."

Her eyes flare as I massage her ass.

"What do you want?"

She blinks up at me and I worry I pushed her too far. Dakota is feisty and stubborn, but she's also hiding insecurities about her body and men.

Her insecurities about her body are easy to deal with. I plan to worship her body as often as she'll allow. Until she knows how crazy she makes me.

Her insecurities about men aren't as easily handled. Her dead husband screwed with her ability to trust men. It'll take time for her to trust a man again. For Dakota, I'm willing to try to be patient.

"You," she finally whispers and I have to lock my muscles before I pounce on her.

My cock protests. It heard green light and it's ready to sink deep into Dakota's warmth before pounding in and out of her until it explodes.

I inhale a deep breath before I listen to my cock. My body is not in charge here. I am.

I brush her wet hair from her face. "You have to tell me exactly what you want or I'm going to flip you over and bend you over this sofa."

She shivers. "And then what?"

"And then I'm going to sink my cock into you while staring at your ass. Maybe I'll slap it."

"No one's ever slapped me before."

"Havoc, I'd be proud to be your first."

"Okay."

"Okay?"

She nods. "Okay. Bend me over the sofa."

I nearly come at those words. I recite multiplication tables until I'm certain I'm not going to explode in my jeans.

"First, I'm going to strip you. Raise your hands."

As soon as her hands are in the air, I rip her t-shirt off of her. Shit. She's still wearing her one-piece swimsuit under her clothes. I fiddle with the straps as I try and figure out how to get this thing off of her.

She giggles. "Do you want me to do it for you?"

"I don't think I have a choice. Your swimsuit appears more complicated than derivatives." I give her some space.

She pushes her jeans down her legs and I can't help myself from staring at her cleavage as she bends over. I've always been a breast man and Dakota has a magnificent pair. I plan to fuck them some day. She kicks off her shoes and jeans before grasping her swimsuit straps. She pulls them down her arms until her breasts pop out.

I reach for her but she shakes her head. "I'll be naked in a jiff."

Naked trumps topless. I drop my hand.

She tugs the straps down her body as she squirms this way and that until the swimsuit is a rolled up lump of wet material at her feet. "Tada."

I pounce. I haul her to me before melding my lips to hers. She sighs and I thrust my tongue inside. I thread a hand through her hair as I explore her mouth. I want to devour her. Touch every inch of her mouth. Memorize each spot that has her wriggling in my arms.

Dakota reaches between us to snap my jeans open. She sticks her hand inside my swimming trunks and wraps a hand around my cock. I moan as she squeezes me.

I enjoy her hand around me for a few pumps before I shackle her wrist to stop her. "No."

"No?" She pouts.

"I want to come when I'm inside you. Don't you want me inside you?" Her eyes flare and I continue. "Pounding into your pussy. Filling you up until you can't tell where I end and you begin. Making you see stars and scream my name."

"I'm not a screamer."

I smirk. "Challenge accepted."

I pull her hand away from me so I can unzip my jeans and push my clothes down. Fuck. Condom. I nearly forgot. I reach for my jeans.

"What are you doing? Are you getting dressed again?"

"Need a condom," I mutter as I dig through my pockets.

Dakota stops me with a hand on my shoulder. "No, you don't."

I glance up at her. Her cheeks flare. "I'm on birth control and I haven't been with anyone else but you in the past year. And I got tested after I found out my dead husband cheated on me with hookers."

"Are you sure?"

"I'm trusting you." She doesn't trust me completely yet but she will. I'll prove to her I'm trustworthy.

I press a hard kiss against her mouth. "The first time is going to be quick."

"I thought you were going to make me scream," she sasses.

"Don't worry. You'll scream," I grumble.

I grasp her hips and spin her around. I place a hand between her shoulder blades and press until she's bent over the sofa. "Widen your legs."

She doesn't hesitate to follow my direction. Perfect. She's fucking perfect.

I notch my cock at her entrance before sinking into her. Fuck. She feels better than anything I've ever felt before. I thought I was addicted to Dakota before.

I was wrong.

Now, I'm addicted.

Chapter 24

"I didn't know what I was missing before. But now I do. Holy mer-cow." ~ Dakota

DAKOTA

Rhett's arm around my waist tightens as he snuggles into my back.

"Did you just smell my hair?"

"It smells of strawberries."

"I'll take your answer as 'yes, I'm a weirdo who smells girls' hair'."

"Not any girl. Only you."

Warmth spreads throughout my body at his words. *Only me.* Little old me. Poor with a broken down car and more debt than any one person can pay off in a lifetime.

"I'm not with you for your money." The words burst from me before my brain can go online and tell me to shut up.

"What?"

I slap a hand over my mouth. No more talking from me.

He rolls me over until we're facing each other and brushes the hair off of my face. "Dakota, I know you're not with me for my money."

"I know. I know. I don't know where those words came from."

He frowns. "I do. You find it difficult to trust men after what happened with your former husband."

"Dead husband," I correct. Former husband sounds too nice considering what he did. How he screwed me from the afterlife. I hope he's enjoying hell.

"Considering what your *dead* husband did, it's normal for you to have trust issues."

I sigh. "I hate it. I hate how stupid I was. How naïve I was. He catfished me, and I told him I loved him."

Rhett growls. "That's the last time you say you loved your dead husband when you're in bed with me."

My eyes widen in confusion. "Are you mad?"

He blows out a breath. "I'm not mad."

If he's not mad, then why did he growl? There's only one other reason I can think of. But it can't be true. I ask anyway. "Are you jealous?"

He scowls.

I point to his face. "That's not no. Holy bananas, you're jealous."

"I don't enjoy the idea of anyone else touching what's mine."

"What's yours? I don't belong to you."

He captures my hand and places it against his heart. "I belong to you, so it's only fair if you belong to me."

"Y-y-you belong to me?"

"I don't want anyone else. Just you."

"You want to be exclusive?"

"Hell, yeah, I do. I don't want any other men touching you."

I giggle. "No other men want to touch me."

He frowns. "Every other man on the beach yesterday wanted you."

I roll my eyes. "Exaggerate much?"

His gaze dips to my chest. "You were running around in a wet swimsuit that clung to all of your delicious curves. I'm not exaggerating."

"Delicious curves? No one's claimed my curves are delicious before."

"You weren't speaking to the right people."

I can't argue with him there. Adam was not the right man. I blame myself for the entire fiasco. I was terrified when I left care. I had two hundred dollars and a bus pass to my name and nowhere to live. I jumped at the chance to move in with him.

I caress Rhett's chest and his heartbeat speeds up in response. A sense of power fills me. It gives me the strength I need to continue the conversation.

"You said exclusive."

He nods. "I did."

"Does this mean we're in a relationship?"

He squeezes my hand. "Havoc, I've wanted to be in a relationship with you since the night in our hotel room in Atlanta."

"You have?"

"But I knew you were scared. It was pretty obvious when you fled the hotel room and jumped on the first flight out of Atlanta."

"It wasn't the first flight."

He grins. "And then you refused to date me."

"You stalked me and wouldn't let me say no."

He shrugs. "I know what I want. I'm not letting you slip through my fingers."

My heart pounds in my chest. He's saying all the right things, but I can't believe him. I can't trust him. I can't trust myself to make the right choice when it comes to men. See aforementioned dead husband who enjoyed hookers a little too much.

Rhett palms my face. "It's okay. I'll wait until you're ready."

He's always waiting for me. At some point, he's going to get tired of waiting. And then I'll lose out on the best thing to ever happen to me. I open my mouth and leap.

"I'm ready."

"You are?"

I nod. "Yes. I'm ready to be in an exclusive relationship with you."

I lock my muscles to stop myself from jumping off of the bed and running away, never to return to this room or hotel or island ever again. I can do this. I've done more difficult things.

Rhett's smile stretches from ear to ear. "There's my brave girl. I think I should reward you."

Tingles explode at his deep voice. "Reward me how?"

"I want to taste you."

I bite my bottom lip. I haven't let him go down on me as I find the act too intimate. It sounds weird since he's been inside me and we're lying here naked together, but oral sex is different. It requires a different level of trust to open yourself wide to a man and let him lick you.

"Okay."

He chuckles. "You're supposed to feel excitement, not trepidation. I can wait to taste you."

"I want to try."

He studies my face for a moment before nodding. "Okay, but if at any time you feel uncomfortable, tell me to stop and I will."

"Do we need a safe word?"

"A safe word?"

"What about chicken?"

He narrows his eyes. "Are you seriously making fun of my relationship with Captain Cluck now?"

I cough to hide my smile. "You have a relationship with a chicken?"

He tickles my ribs. "Make fun of me, will you?"

"Stop! Stop!" I manage to say between my bursts of laughter.

He rolls on top of me. "You're beautiful, Havoc."

I feel beautiful when he looks at me as if he can't believe he's in this bed with me. It's the most empowering feeling I've ever experienced.

"You ready to come for me?"

I bite my lip. I've never orgasmed during oral sex before. "Maybe."

"Challenge accepted," Rhett murmurs, his voice thick with promise. He slides down my body, his breath warm against my skin, until his face hovers between my thighs. He inhales deeply. "Strawberries."

A shiver runs through me as his hands glide up and down my inner thighs, slow and deliberate. "Widen for me, Havoc."

I exhale and remind myself this is Rhett – the man who sees me, who thinks I'm beautiful. The man who's given me more pleasure in two encounters than Adam did in an entire year. I part my thighs.

"Good girl." His voice is a low rumble as he settles between my thighs, his broad shoulders pressing them wider.

Then, his tongue flicks over my clit and a bolt of pleasure shoots through me. Oh. My. God. Maybe I was wrong about oral sex.

He wraps his lips around my clit and sucks, and my back arches off the bed as if pulled by an unseen force. Rhett chuckles before pressing an arm over my waist to hold me in place.

A teasing finger traces my entrance as his tongue works me over, sending waves of heat rolling through my belly. I need more. I need him inside me.

"Rhett," I moan. I sound desperate. I feel desperate.

His lips curl into a smirk against my skin. "Something you want?"

A shiver racks my body. Holy sex gods. Rhett knows exactly what he's doing.

"You. I want you."

"I'm right here, Havoc," he murmurs, but his fingers remain maddeningly still.

"Stop teasing me."

"Tell me what you want."

My breath hitches. "Your fingers."

The words barely leave my lips before he thrusts two fingers deep inside me. A strangled gasp escapes me as he works them in and out, matching the rhythm of his tongue on my clit.

"I can't… I'm…" My words slip away as my thoughts unravel. All that matters is this moment.

"Come for me." Rhett's voice is a rough command against my skin, and I shatter, pleasure crashing over me in relentless waves.

He doesn't stop. Not until I'm nothing but a boneless heap against the sheets, the last tingles of my orgasm ebbing into blissful exhaustion. I was definitely wrong about oral sex.

I manage a breathless, "We're doing that again."

Rhett chuckles. "I've created a monster."

Chapter 25

"Who knew work could be this fun?" ~ Rhett

RHETT

"Are you serious? You want us to walk into the office separately?"

Dakota nods. "Yes."

"My brothers know we're dating. You came with me to *Barnacles & Barnyards.*"

"How is Captain Cluck anyway?"

I scowl at her, but I'm not serious. It's cute how she teases me. She giggles.

She bats her eyelashes at me. "What's wrong? Paradise with your Captain not working out the way you planned?"

"You'll pay for that."

"Oh no. What are you going to do? Spank me?"

"Maybe."

"Please. You keep saying you will, but you never do. I'm starting to think you're a liar."

My cock twitches and I nearly moan at the idea of her ass with my red handprint on it. "Keep teasing me and you'll find out I'm not a liar while we're at work."

She gasps. "Rhett Raider. Wait. Do you have a middle name?"

"No. My dad didn't believe in middle names."

Her brow wrinkles. "Believe in middle names? It's not a religion you can question the existence of. It's a name in between your first and last one."

I shrug. "Nonetheless. I don't have a middle name."

She clears her throat. "Okay. Rhett Raider, you are not going to get up to any sexy shenanigans in the office. I am serious about my job. I'm not putting it in jeopardy."

"Not even a little kiss in the break room?"

"No kissing. No petting. Definitely, no nudity."

"Eli had sex with Paisley in her office numerous times when the brewery was temporarily housed here."

She holds up a finger. "One, I don't have an office and I'm not into public nudity." She adds a finger. "And, two, Eli's a billionaire. He can do whatever he wants."

"I'm part—"

She doesn't allow me to finish explaining how I'm part owner of the distillery before she flashes me a third finger. "And, three, Paisley didn't work for the distillery."

"Neither do you."

"I work for Eli, who owns the distillery. Therefore, I pretty much work for the distillery."

I chuckle. "I give up. I'm not going to win this argument with you."

"It's good you realize when you're beaten."

"But I'm not entering the office separately. I'm not ashamed of you."

"Rhett Raider – your name has a nice ring to it. I do love alliteration – you better not be ashamed of me."

"I literally said I wasn't two seconds ago."

"Good."

Dakota can talk circles around me. Before I figure out which way is up, the work day will be over. I'm not Miles or Zane. I'm serious about ensuring *Buccaneer's Whiskey and Distillery* is a financial success.

One day, I hope to be able to hand the reins of the company over to my children. Children, I hope, will have green eyes and blonde, curly hair. The thought has me smiling as I slam my door shut and walk around to open Dakota's door for her.

"Do you want children?"

Her eyes widen, and she rears back. "You did not ask me about children right before we start work. You're a menace, Rhett Raider. And I've changed my mind. Rhett Raider is too long. You're RR from now on."

I throw an arm over her shoulders as we walk to the office entrance. She tries to shrug me off but I don't let her. I want her to understand I'm serious about us. I'm not pretending we're not involved just because we're at work. Fuck that.

As soon as we're inside, she scoots away from me and rushes to her desk. "Did you notice the time? We're late."

We wouldn't have been late if she hadn't pushed her ass against my morning hard-on. The sexy mink.

I catch her at her desk and whirl her around. I drop a hard kiss to her mouth before retreating. "See you later, Havoc."

She huffs at me and I stroll to my office whistling. Time to make up for months of frustration when I didn't have Dakota.

I settle behind my desk. While my computer starts up, I type a message to Dakota.

Excuse me, ma'am. I'm looking for a gorgeous, highly intelligent woman with an unfortunate attraction to her cocky coworker. Have you seen her?

I think you have the wrong number.

Impossible. She was last seen rolling her eyes at me and pretending she isn't thinking about what I'd do to her if we were alone in this office.

Sounds like a real HR violation.

Only if we get caught.

"Get to work, RR," she shouts from her desk in the reception area.

I chuckle as I throw my phone on my desk and open my email.

Thirty minutes later, I find myself reaching for my phone again. *I need to borrow your stapler.*

You couldn't come up with a better excuse?

Fine. I need to staple some papers, but honestly, I also need to see you bite your lip in frustration when I 'accidentally' brush against you.

You are ridiculous.

And yet, here you are, smiling at your phone like you secretly love it.

She glances behind her and notices me standing in the hallway. I wave at her. She shoos me away. "Go back to your desk, perv!"

I salute her before spinning around. I throw my phone into a drawer. It's too tempting to tease Dakota, and I really do need to get some work done.

Some time later, my stomach growls to remind me it's nearly time for lunch. Excellent. Time to convince Dakota to go home for 'lunch' with me.

"Dakota," I holler down the hallway. "I need to see you."

Zane pokes his head in my office. "What do you need Dakota for?"

"Yea," Miles says as he joins him. "What do you need Dakota for?"

I glare at my younger brothers. "None of your damn business."

"I bet he wants to bend her over her desk," Miles says.

"Or have her sit on his lap," Zane says.

I growl as I stalk toward them. "You will not make fun of Dakota."

"It's okay," Dakota says from behind them. "I get it. They're jealous."

"I'm not jealous," Miles says and Zane nods his agreement.

"Oh really?" Dakota crosses her arms over her chest. "And I didn't overhear you saying what a lucky bastard Rhett is."

I am a lucky bastard.

Miles scowls. "Maybe I was referring to something else."

She lifts her eyebrows. "Such as his relationship with Captain Cranky?"

I groan. I am never going to hear the end of how some stupid chicken sat on my shoulder all morning at the petting zoo.

"Did someone say Captain Cranky?" Kai asks as he joins us.

"Is no one working?" I ask.

"Jaxon is. The man doesn't know how to stop. He's a machine." Kai feigns retching.

"And Eli's working, too." Miles points to Eli's office door, which is shut.

Zane snorts. "Sure, he's 'working'. Paisley snuck in there fifteen minutes ago."

Miles rubs his hands together. "Excellent. We should create an emergency and disturb them."

Dakota raises her hands. "You're on your own with this one."

Zane pouts. "But you're excellent at pranks."

She grins. "I am. But I don't need to see my boss's naked ass ever again."

I growl. "When did you see Eli's naked ass?"

"When I walked in on him with Paisley bent over his desk." She shivers. "I learned to knock on his door awful quick."

"Welp. If we're not pranking Eli, let's go get some lunch," Kai says.

"Awesome. I'm starving." Miles rubs his belly.

Dakota's stomach growls and her eyes widen as she slams a hand over her middle.

Zane throws an arm over her shoulders. "Little sis is hungry, too."

"Little?" Dakota asks.

"You may be older but you're height challenged."

She glares at him. "I am not short."

"Didn't say you were. I used the term height challenged. It's more inclusive. You should try it."

She elbows him and he yelps as he releases her. "I am not height challenged. The Raider brothers are abnormally tall." She studies Zane. "Is it to compensate for other shortcomings?"

"Uh oh." Kai shakes his head at me. "You've disappointed her in bed."

My gaze meets Dakota's. "Is this the hill you want to die on? Claiming I disappointed you in bed?"

Her cheeks darken. "I didn't say anything of the sort! It was Kai!"

"Come on." Miles herds her out of my office and down the hallway. "Let's discuss this over lunch."

"You better be buying," she mutters.

"Big brother's buying. Apparently, he has stuff to make up for." Miles winks at her.

I guess we're going to lunch together. So much for my plans to take Dakota to my house, strip her naked, and make her come twice before returning to the office.

But there's no way I'm tearing her away from having fun with my brothers. She's never experienced having siblings before. She can borrow mine whenever she wants.

Maybe forever.

Chapter 26

"Otters are adorable. Fight me on this." ~ Dakota

DAKOTA

I crane my neck to stare up at Rhett's house through the windshield of his SUV. "Wowzer."

He chuckles. "Wowzer?"

"Your house has left me speechless."

"And you went with wowzer?"

I slap his shoulder. "Knock it off. I've never been in a house this fancy before."

He immediately sobers. "Sorry. I forgot."

"Ugh. Don't say sorry every time my background growing up in care comes up. It's not your fault. And I don't need your pity."

"Pity? I don't pity you. How could I pity the strongest woman I know?"

I roll my eyes. "There's no need to flatter me. I'm a sure thing."

He reaches across the console and grabs me. I yelp but it doesn't stop him from dragging me onto his lap and wedging me between him and the steering wheel.

"Is it 'demonstrate your strength' day?"

He hits a button and his seat moves until my back isn't jammed against the steering wheel. He cradles my face in his hands. "I'm not trying to flatter you, Havoc. You are one of the strongest women I know."

"I don't feel very strong. I feel exhausted from working for Eli all day long and then working the graveyard shift at the *Mermaid Motel*. And, despite all the work, I'm still barely earning enough money to pay off all my debts."

"Let me help you. I don't have to give you the money. You can borrow it."

"No." I shake my head. "I can barely make the loan payments I have now."

"I'll lower the loan payments."

"And then I'll be paying you until I'm 162 years old."

He chuckles. "Planning on living a long life?"

I lock my muscles before I flinch. I hope to live a long life – I'm doing everything within my power to ensure it – but the cards are stacked against me.

I roll my eyes and feign nonchalance. "I'm going to have to if I pay any less money on my loan payments."

He leans his forehead against mine. "I wish you'd let me pay off your loans."

"It's good to want."

He grunts. "I'm not going to win this argument."

He wasn't asking but I say, "Nope," anyway.

He opens the door and lifts me off of his lap and sets me on my feet. I was right. It is 'demonstrate your strength' day. You won't hear me complaining. Any excuse to watch Rhett's muscles bunch and strain is a good day in my opinion.

"Come on." He entwines his fingers with mine and leads me to the house.

I study the structure as we get closer. I wasn't kidding about it being fancy. It reminds me of a postcard of a typical island house – bright white with deep blue shutters, a wraparound porch framed by thick wooden columns, and a set of wide steps leading up to the grand mahogany front door.

I glide my hand along the railing as we ascend the stairs to the porch. On one side, a set of rocking chairs faces the water. Perfect for lazy afternoons with a glass of lemonade. Further around, a hanging daybed sways slightly in the breeze.

I sigh. "I've always wanted a front porch with a swing on it."

"You can borrow my porch whenever you want."

"I'll pencil you in for a late supper since it's the only free time I have for the next decade or so." He scowls and I backpedal. "I'm sorry. I'll stop bringing up how much I work now. It's boring."

"Nothing about you is boring."

"Ha! You haven't seen my everyday panties."

His eyes flare.

I shake my head. "All you heard was panties."

He shrugs. "I'm a man standing in front of a sexy woman. What do you expect?"

I motion to the door. "For you to show me inside."

He unlocks the door. Stepping inside, I feel as if I'm walking straight into an architectural magazine titled *Houses Too Nice for People Who Are Accident Prone.* The open-concept space stretches before us in a perfect blend of elegance and easy coastal charm. Sunlight pours through floor-to-ceiling windows, glinting off the rich hardwood floors and bouncing off the high, exposed-beam ceilings.

To the left, is a sleek, modern kitchen straight out of a cooking show. It boasts marble countertops and top-of-the-line appliances, all of which I will absolutely never use but will admire from a safe distance. The dining area features a massive reclaimed-wood table. And the living room? It's the kind of space that invites you to curl up on a plush white sofa – if you aren't terrified of spilling coffee on it.

"Wowzer times two."

Rhett wraps his arms around my waist from behind and rests his chin on my shoulder. "You like it?"

"Are you seriously asking? It's gorgeous." I throw out my arm. "It's obviously not a cheap place, but it's inviting. Not cold."

He kisses my neck before releasing me. "I'm glad you approve since I plan for you to spend more time here."

"Here?" I point to the floor. "Or in the bedroom."

His eyes flash. "Oh, Havoc, I don't need a bedroom to make you scream."

"We've been over this. I don't scream."

He chuckles. "Liar. I can…" He trails off.

"You can what?"

He stalks toward the kitchen. "I saw movement."

"Do you have a cat? I'm more of a dog person myself but cats are okay, too."

"I don't have a cat," he mumbles as he kneels in front of the kitchen island.

"Bummer," I mutter. "I can't have an animal at the hotel. I don't really have the time to care for one but a cat doesn't need tons of cuddles."

"There!" He jumps to his feet and rushes to the corner.

I hurry after him. "What is it?"

A brown lump of fur is cowering in the corner.

"It's a rat." Rhett tries to pick it up but it swipes a paw at him.

"It's not a rat. It's Viking." I kneel in front of her. "Hi, Viking. How did you get in here?"

The poor otter shakes as she stares up at me with big, brown eyes.

"Do you have any cookies? I need a cookie."

"You need a cookie now?" Rhett asks.

I push him toward one of the doors. "Go look in the pantry. I assume you have a pantry. You must have something sweet. She prefers chocolate."

"She? Am I searching for cookies for the otter?"

"Duh. She's probably hungry. Who knows how long she's been stuck in here."

Rhett swears under his breath as he opens the pantry door and pulls out a bag of chocolate chip cookies. He hands me the bag. I rip it open, and suddenly I have an otter on my lap.

"Oh, poor baby. You're starving." I feed her pieces of a cookie as I chatter away to her. "How did you get in here anyway? Are you lost? Does Parker know where you are? We should phone her to let her know you're fine. Do you want to stay with us tonight?"

"Stay with us tonight?" Rhett asks.

"Only until ten. I'll drop her off at Parker's on my way to the hotel." She finishes up the cookie but I don't give her more. I probably shouldn't be feeding an otter chocolate chip cookies in the first place.

I stand with her in my arms. "How do you think she got in here?" I ask as I rock her back and forth.

"My asshole brothers."

"What?"

As if on cue, the door bursts open and his brothers pile inside. "One. Two. Three. Four. We declare a prank war!"

Rhett crosses his arms over his chest and glares at them. "You need five siblings to declare a prank war."

Kai waves his phone in the air. "We have a power of attorney from Eli."

I giggle. "You have a power of attorney from Eli in order to declare a prank war?"

Jaxon pushes his glasses up his nose. "Apparently, only one power of attorney is allowed, so I got stuck coming here."

Zane elbows him. "You need to spend more time with us. You're getting boring."

Miles snorts. "Getting?"

"You declared your prank war. Now, get out of here." Rhett tries to herd them toward the door but no one moves.

"You know the rules. You get pranked. You buy everyone dinner," Kai says.

Jaxon sighs. "Can't we make an exception? I'm working on a new whiskey flavor."

"All exceptions need agreement from five brothers," Zane says.

Jaxon and Rhett raise their hands. "Exception!"

"No exception," Kai, Zane, and Miles say in unison.

"Fine." Rhett huffs. "Go to whatever restaurant you want and put it on my tab."

Miles collapses on Rhett's sofa. "I already ordered takeout."

Rhett growls and I pat his chest. "What's the big deal? It's a family dinner."

He leans close to whisper in my ear. "My brothers are cock-blockers."

I shiver at the feel of his breath against my skin. "Do you want me to kick them out? We can eat together some other time."

He sighs. "No. I want you to enjoy spending time with a family."

"Good. Because I'm not leaving this guy alone anyway." I lift Viking in front of his face. "And I don't want him watching us. He'd be scandalized."

He chuckles. "You obviously haven't heard the story about Viking and the cat."

The doorbell rings and Miles rushes to answer it. "Pizza!"

Rhett grabs plates and silverware from the kitchen and I help him set the table. It's a simple domestic task. A task thousands of couples perform every day. But it makes me feel all warm and gooey inside to work beside Rhett while his brothers fool around.

I'm falling hard and fast for Rhett. And his family, too.

Chapter 27

"Drunk guests have their uses." ~ Dakota

DAKOTA

Rhett pulls to a stop in front of the motel.

"I could have driven myself. You didn't have to drop me off."

He squeezes my thigh. "It's no trouble."

"Except you now have to pick me up in the morning since my car's still at the distillery."

"I don't mind."

I narrow my eyes on him. "Admit it. You hate Matilda."

"Matilda needs to retire."

"Matilda got me to the island." Barely. But she made it here.

"Your car is not safe."

"Matilda is perfectly safe. Besides, you know I can't afford to buy a new car now."

Shame tries to lift its head, but I push it down. I will not be ashamed of being in financial trouble. I'm proud of how hard I'm working to pay off my debts. The reason I have those debts? That's a bit shameful, but I'm ignoring my past.

"Hmm…" He drums his fingers on the steering wheel.

I can practically see the wheels turning in his mind. "No way."

He bats his eyes – the picture of innocence. "No way, what?"

"No way are you buying me a car."

"Just a small one for your birthday."

Rhett has lost all touch with reality. "You don't buy a car as a birthday present. Besides, my birthday is months away."

He grunts. "You're being unreasonable."

I clutch my chest. "Me? I'm the one being unreasonable? Because I'm not letting you buy me a car?"

"Exactly."

"I'm not with you for your money, RR."

"I know. But it doesn't change the fact that I do have money."

I almost wish he didn't. It would make our relationship more equal. I feel as if he holds all the cards now. He has money and a family. I have neither of those.

"I need to get to work." My shift begins in five minutes, and it's a great excuse to get out of this conversation.

He folds out of the SUV and walks around to open my door for me. I try to scramble out before he can help me, but he grasps my hips to stop me.

"I worry about you when you're driving. Your car isn't safe."

Ugh. He pulled the worry card. I don't want him to worry about me. "I only drive from the motel to the distillery. It's ten minutes max."

"A car can crash in less than ten minutes."

I flinch. I'm aware of how quickly a car crash can end someone's life.

"Fuck. I'm sorry, Havoc. I shouldn't have mentioned a car crash."

"It's okay."

He palms my neck and draws me near until he can wrap his arms around me. "It's not okay. It was an asshole move reminding you of your husband's accident to try and manipulate you."

I allow myself to enjoy his comfort for a few seconds before I push away. "I really do need to get to work."

He frowns and I hold up my hand. "Don't you dare say you'll pay off my loans. Especially not when Ms. Nosey is watching us." I point to Sadie, standing at the entrance of the motel, spying on us. She waves in response.

Rhett kisses my nose. "I'll pick you up in the morning for work."

I watch as he drives away. I need to figure out the car situation before he buys me a new one. If I give in on the car, he'll pay off my loans, too. They're not his loans to pay off. I don't need a man to handle my problems for me.

"What were you guys talking about?" Sadie asks as she opens the door for me. "It looked tense."

I scowl at her. "You're not going to pretend you weren't watching?"

"Why? We both know I was spying."

Despite myself, I smile. "You're crazy."

"You obviously haven't spent a lot of time with other people on Smuggler's Hideaway. I'm boring compared to most of them."

"I want to disagree with you, but I just rescued an otter from the Raider brothers."

"I knew they were the ones who stole Viking! Parker was completely panicked. She called every business in Smuggler's Rest. She was convinced Viking escaped the bakery while she was taking out the trash."

Kai, Zane, or Miles could have told her they were borrowing the otter for a prank. There was no reason to let her panic. They need to learn some manners and I'm up for the task. Especially after they got into a food fight at dinner. They weren't the ones cleaning up the mess.

"Parker's okay now. We dropped Viking off with her before Rhett brought me here."

She rubs her hands together. "And we're back to the hottie. Tell me more. Did he bring you to his house and make you see stars?"

I did see his house and I thought he was going to make me see stars, but then his brothers showed up and ruined our plans. All of which is none of Ms. Nosey's business.

"Don't you have mail to chase after?" I ask as I make my way to the reception desk. A wave of dizziness hits me and I clutch the desk before I collapse on the floor. Once the dizziness has receded, I grab a juice box from my bag and drink from it.

"Are you okay?" Sadie asks.

"Fine." I wave away her concern.

She narrows her eyes on me. "You aren't pregnant, are you?"

My mouth drops open. "Pregnant?"

She shrugs. "Some women have dizzy spells when they're pregnant."

"No, I'm not pregnant." In fact, I don't plan to have children. The doctors claim it's possible for me to have a healthy child but considering how I was born, I won't risk it.

I haven't told Rhett I don't want children yet. Based on some of his throwaway comments, he wants kids. I'm afraid of how he'll react to my not wanting any.

"Bummer. Those Raider men are sexy as all get out. I bet their babies will be gorgeous."

"Why are you so interested in the Raider brothers? I thought you had your own thing going on."

"No Raider brother for me," she says and ignores my attempt to find out what's got her buzzing with excitement every time the mail is delivered. "My sister dated one and it did not end well. No, thank you."

"Who did your sister date?"

"Miles."

"I get how dating him could be heartbreaking." Miles is sweet and charming, but he doesn't take anything in life seriously. Except surfing. I wouldn't handle coming in second to a surfboard very well.

She sighs. "Hazel never got over him."

"That sucks."

"Men suck."

"Preaching to the choir, sister."

Her nose wrinkles. "What do you mean? Rhett is a perfect gentleman with you." She leans on the desk as if she's settling in for a chat. She's going to be disappointed. I'm not telling her about Adam any more than I'd tell her about my sex life with Rhett.

There's a commotion outside and I glance out of the window. A group of men stumble their way toward the hotel.

"I love mermaids!" one of them shouts right before he runs head-on into the door, rears back, and lands on his ass.

His friends try to help him up but they're laughing too hard to be of any assistance. I go to help but before I manage to reach them, they end up splayed on the sidewalk.

"We should abandon them here," Sadie says as we stare down at the group.

"The stars are beautiful on this island."

"The mermaids are even better."

"Dude. Mermaids aren't real."

"Those seashell bras felt awful real."

"Don't lie. You didn't feel a thing."

"She rejected you."

"And somehow we all ended up drinking shots of moonshine."

"Visitors can't handle Smuggler's Hideaway moonshine," Sadie mutters before clapping her hands to get their attention. "Okay, boys. You have two choices here. Get your asses up and get to your room. Or get run over since you're laying in the parking lot."

"No wonder this bed isn't comfortable," one of them says before stumbling to his feet. He sways but manages to stay upright.

Sadie and I help the other two men to stand. One of the men wraps an arm around me and leans into me. I nearly fall over from his weight.

Somehow, we manage to get the men into the motel and up the stairs to their room. They can't find their key but I open the door with the master.

"I'll alert housekeeping they'll need extra time with their room tomorrow," I say once the men are tucked away in their room.

Sadie skips down the steps and toward the door. She spins around before she reaches it to wag a finger at me. "We'll discuss your bad experience with men tomorrow."

Darn. I thought I got away with avoiding the conversation. I'll have to think up some excuse tomorrow.

Chapter 28

"My brothers are assholes." ~ Rhett

RHETT

"Where are we going?" Dakota asks as I drive away from the *Mermaid Motel.*

I drum my fingers on the steering wheel as I contemplate how to answer. Will she go running back to the motel screaming if I tell her the truth before we arrive?

"You have camping gear in the backseat. Are we going camping?"

Damn. I should have put the gear in the rear. "Kind of."

"Rhett Raider, tell me where we're going this minute."

"Uh oh. The last name treatment. I'm in trouble now." I pause and decide to take a chance. "Have you heard of the Smuggler's Grotto?"

"No. Tell me. Smuggler's Hideaway is fascinating." She tucks her right ankle under her left knee and settles in to listen.

I'm glad she enjoys Smuggler's Hideaway, because if I have it my way, she won't be leaving the island anytime soon.

"Smuggler's Grotto is a hidden cave system beneath the island. According to legend, it was used by pirates and later by Prohibition-era rumrunners."

"Really? Sounds cool. I'm surprised I haven't heard of it. The motel guests are always asking about touristy things to visit."

I squirm in my seat. "There's a catch."

"A catch? What kind of catch? Is it part of a magical system and you need a wand to enter?"

I chuckle. "A wand to enter?"

She shrugs. "I fell asleep watching Harry Potter last night."

"No magical system, although." I pause. This next part may freak her out. "It's supposedly haunted by ghosts of betrayed smugglers who still guard their stolen treasure."

"Haunted? I'm surprised there weren't organized tours during the *Ghost Tide Festival.*"

"The area isn't safe enough for tours."

She lifts a brow. "And yet we're going there?"

I frown. "Because I don't have a choice."

"You don't have a choice? Is someone holding a gun to your head?" She checks the backseat for any stragglers. "Unless they're invisible, I don't see anyone."

"Since my asshole brothers managed to sneak Viking into my house, I'm losing the prank war," I mutter.

"And your punishment is visiting the Smuggler's Grotto."

"My punishment is spending the night in the grotto," I correct.

Her eyes widen. "We're going to spend the night in a haunted grotto?"

"Yes?" I hold my breath as I wait for her response. Most women don't want to spend the night sleeping in a sleeping bag on the floor of a damp and dreary cave.

She shivers. Damnit. She's scared. What am I doing? Dragging her into this prank war with my brothers? I should have left her alone for her night off. But she gets so few nights off. I didn't want to miss one with her.

"Okay." She blows out a breath. "I can't lie and say I'm excited to spend the night in a grotto, but I trust you."

Warmth fills my stomach. Dakota trusts me. I know how hard it is for her to trust after what her asshole dead husband did to her. But she trusts me.

Dakota is not like other women. She's unique. She's the woman I want to spend my life with.

Whoa. Where did that thought come from? I never planned to spend my life with a woman. Because I didn't think I could trust one. I never thought I could trust a woman enough to want to spend my life with her.

But I trust Dakota. She's poured her heart out to me. She's the strongest woman I know.

And she trusts me. A feeling of contentment settles over me. As if all the pieces of a puzzle are falling into place.

"Wait until you find out about the lover's curse," I say as I park my SUV at the parking lot for a small beach on the Southern side of the island.

I exit the vehicle and walk around the front to Dakota's door. She's already out and gathering the camping equipment.

I snatch one sleeping bag, the cooler, and the lantern from her hands.

"You can carry one sleeping bag."

She rolls her eyes. "Mr. Control strikes again."

I press a hard kiss to her lips. "You enjoy it when I'm in control."

Her eyes flare, but she plants a hand on her hip. "Not all the time," she sasses.

"I guess I need to work harder then."

She bites her bottom lip and I groan. "Do not get me hard."

She bats her eyelashes. "Why not? Don't you want me?"

"Minx," I groan. "I want you. I always want you. I'm going to be old and grey and unable to get a hard-on and want you."

She giggles. "How can you want me if you can't get a hard-on?"

"It's called a little blue pill."

"Do you need a little blue pill now?"

I glare down at her. "I'll show you I don't need a little blue pill."

"Yea!"

"But not tonight."

She curls her bottom lip in a pout. "But it's my night off."

"It's also the night of my punishment for losing in the prank war." I nod toward the beach. "Follow me."

"What does sleeping in the grotto for punishment have to do with anything?"

"My brothers aren't going to leave us alone tonight," I explain as we walk through the sand toward the cave. "And I don't want to have to kill one of them for watching you when you come."

She grimaces. "I hate to agree with you."

"But I'm right."

She growls. It's adorable. "Don't let it get to your head, Mr. High and Mighty."

"I thought I was Mr. Control."

"You can be both."

We reach a rocky outcrop, and I stop. "You have to crawl to get inside the cave."

She motions to the rocks. "Lead the way."

I grab the sleeping bag from her and crouch down. I place the sleeping bags on the cooler and push it in front of me as I make my way through the rock formations, hiding the cave from the naked eye. As soon as I reach the entrance, I whirl around and pull Dakota into the cave.

"Wow." She scans the area. "It's huge."

She shivers and I nudge her toward the center of the cave where a fire pit is. I wipe off one of the logs and help her to sit before unrolling the sleeping bag and placing it over her shoulders.

"Tell me about the lover's curse."

I switch on the lantern and set it next to us. While I get a fire in the pit going, I explain the curse to her.

"Legend has it, the pirate Black Jack was in love with Margaret Hale, the daughter of the lighthouse keeper. When her father discovered their secret affair, he arranged for her to marry a wealthy man instead. On the night of her wedding, Black

Jack kidnapped her, intending to escape the island by boat. But a violent storm rolled in, trapping them inside the grotto. The next morning, only Margaret's body was found – Black Jack had vanished. Some believe he drowned, while others whisper that Margaret's ghost keeps him trapped in the cave, forever doomed to roam."

Dakota sighs. "How romantic."

I groan. "No, you can't be into ghosts."

"Why not?"

"Because between you and my brothers, I'll never win another prank war."

"You need to try harder. I can think of a bunch of pranks."

I narrow my eyes on her. "No more pranking me by messing with my keyboard."

She wags her finger at me. "As long as you behave."

I launch myself at her and tickle her ribs. She giggles and I allow the sound of her happiness to fill up all the empty spaces inside me.

"Don't touch her!" someone shouts, and I jump to my feet.

I scan the cave, but I don't see anyone. "Knock it off, Raider brothers!"

"Who are the Raider brothers?" a voice calls back.

"My asshole brothers."

Dakota slaps me. "Don't call them assholes."

"Leave the woman and go," a voice says from behind me.

I whirl around. "I'm not leaving my woman in your clutches."

A spooky laughter rebounds off the cave walls as the area fills with smoke. The distant echo of boots on the rock comes next. It's supposed to sound as if smugglers are moving cargo in the dark. In reality, it's my brothers messing with me.

Dakota giggles, and I glare down at her. She holds up her hands. "Sorry. But this is hilarious."

"What's hilarious about my brothers being assholes?"

"They're not assholes. They're your brothers."

And now I feel like an asshole. Dakota has no family, and here I am complaining about mine. I should be more mindful. I should apologize. Let her know my family is now her family.

"We like her," a voice I happen to know is Miles says.

"We're going to keep her," another voice, I suspect is Zane, says.

Despite how annoying they're being, I smile. My family likes Dakota. She fits right in.

She's mine. There's no denying it anymore. I love this woman. I would do anything to make her happy. Including spending a night in a cave with my brothers pranking us.

"I like your family," Dakota says.

I'm glad because she's stuck with them since I'm not letting her go. I should probably tell her how I feel. But we have time. We have all the time in the world.

Chapter 29

"If you put a dart in my hand, don't be surprised when I hit you with it." ~ Dakota

DAKOTA

Zane skips to a stop in front of my desk. "Come along, little sister."

My heart skips a beat – little sister? Does he consider me family? Before I melt into a pile of happy goo on the floor, I sass at him. "I'm pretty sure I'm older than you."

He pats the top of my head. "But you're cute."

I roll my eyes. "I'll show you how cute I am when I prank you."

He rubs his hands together. "Another prank war? I'm in."

Rhett growls as he pushes Zane away from my desk. "Stop bothering Dakota."

"I'm not bothering her. I'm kidnapping her."

I giggle. "Kidnapping me? Where are we going?"

"It's Friday."

"And?"

Miles strolls into the reception area. "Friday means *Rumrunner*."

"Rumrunner? Are we going to smuggle illegal alcohol? And here I thought *Buccaneer's Whiskey* was a legit business."

"It is a legit business," Rhett insists.

"Color me confused."

Zane picks up a marker from my desk. "Blue okay?"

Rhett slaps the marker out of his hand. "You aren't coloring Dakota's face."

"Spoilsport. I was merely going to draw a little bird on her face."

Rhett crosses his arms over his chest and glares at his younger brother. "A bird? Or the bird?"

Zane shrugs. "Does it matter?"

I open my drawer and throw all of my colored markers in it. Fun is one thing. Having someone draw on your face with permanent marker is another.

The door opens and Kai sticks his head inside. "Are we going or are you going to babble like a bunch of old women all day?"

"We're waiting for Dakota," Miles says.

"Waiting for me?" I'm confused. The brothers don't usually invite me on their escapades.

"You're one of the family now, sis."

My heart doesn't just skip a beat at Miles's explanation. It goes completely bananas, thumping away. I've never had a family before. I thought Adam would be my family. I couldn't have been more wrong.

Am I wrong now? Am I making a mistake? Should I not trust Rhett and his brothers?

Rhett kneels in front of me. "You don't have to go if you don't want to, Havoc. I know my brothers are a bit much to handle."

"Hey!" Kai shouts. "I resemble that remark."

I bite my lip as I study his brothers – Miles, Kai, and Zane. Should I go? Or should I keep my heart safe from this family?

Miles presses his hands together. "Please, Dakota. Please come with."

"Yea." Zane nods. "Big brother will be all grumpy if you don't join us."

"You want me to come with?" I need to be sure.

Kai rolls his eyes. "Of course, we do. You're our little sister. We haven't had one of those before."

"Hey!" Paisley strolls out of Eli's office. "What am I?"

"Smart enough to stay away from these yahoos," Eli says as he follows her.

Kai skips to Paisley. "You're our big sister. Dakota is our little sister."

Eli pushes Kai away from Paisley, and Kai chuckles in response. "You're whipped."

"It's going to be fun watching you fall in love," Eli mutters.

Kai wags a finger at him. "Not my turn." He motions to Rhett and me. "Theirs."

Rhett's hand on my thigh tightens. "Do not scare, Dakota."

I pat his shoulder. "They're not scaring me." They're terrifying me. But in a good way. I stand. "Let's go smuggle some illegal booze."

Paisley giggles. "You fit right in."

"We don't have to go if you don't want to," Rhett insists. "We can spend a quiet evening watching a movie or having a nice dinner."

I kiss his cheek. "I…" I snap my mouth shut. I nearly told Rhett I love him for worrying about me. But I don't love him. I couldn't possibly love him. I know better than to fall for the first man to give me attention after Adam died.

Rhett smiles down at me. "You what?"

My breath gets caught in my throat as those piercing blue eyes concentrate on me. Apparently, I don't know better than to fall in love. Because this man – this controlling man who I swore would never control me – owns my heart.

"I-I-I want to go," I stutter.

His smile widens. "Then, we go."

Eli herds everyone out of the office and soon enough we're walking down an alley in Smuggler's Rest.

"Where are we going?" I ask. "I was joking about smuggling alcohol. I can't get another strike on my record."

Rhett squeezes my hand. "*Rumrunner* is a speakeasy."

Now I remember. Sadie told me about the place ages ago. I nearly forgot. This is so exciting. An honest to goodness speakeasy. This island is the coolest. "Seriously? Do we need a code word?"

He chuckles. "Locals don't need a code word."

"I'm not a local."

He scowls. "You live here. You're a local." He halts and twirls me around until I'm standing in his arms. "Who made you feel unwelcome?"

"Unwelcome?"

"It's okay, Dakota." He brushes the hair out of my face. "You can tell me."

"No one's made me feel unwelcome. Unless we count the time this big grouch knocked on my car window and scared the crap out of me."

He frowns. "I'm sorry, Havoc. I didn't mean to scare you. I was an asshole."

I grin up at him. "It's good you're aware of your asshole tendencies."

"My asshole tendencies. I'll show you my asshole tendencies when I…" He leans down to whisper in my ear. "…don't let you come for a very long time tonight."

I shiver. I'll never admit it out loud, but I love it when he takes control in the bedroom. After being married to Adam, who controlled our finances and therefore thoroughly screwed me over, I'm surprised I can give any man control. But Rhett isn't any man.

"I'm not the only one who won't be coming tonight. I have to work in a few hours."

He growls. "You should let me help you pay your bills."

I roll my eyes. "We've been over this. I can handle my problems myself. I don't need some big, growly man to step in."

"But you admit I'm big."

I roll my eyes. "Such a man."

"Lovebirds!" Miles waves from where he's holding a door open.

I grasp Rhett's hand and drag him toward the door. In my rush, I trip on air and stumble. Rhett catches me before I fall on my face.

"Easy there, Havoc."

I point to the ground. "It came up and bit me."

He chuckles. "Sure, it did."

We step inside the bar and my mouth drops open. This place is cool. Dim lighting flickers from antique sconces and casts a golden hue over the dark wooden interior. The walls are exposed brick, and behind the bar, there are mahogany shelves stacked high with aged liquor bottles. I feel as if I've stepped back in time to the Prohibition.

Paisley captures my hand and tugs me away from Rhett. "You have to see this."

"What?" I ask as I stumble to keep up with her.

She points to the bar. Kai is leaning over it while chatting with the bartender.

"What's happening? What am I watching?"

She giggles. "Kai striking out with the owner, Harper."

I gasp. "It's possible for a Raider brother to strike out?"

She shakes her head. "You've got it bad for Rhett."

I elbow her. "At least his assistant didn't catch us going at it in his office."

Her cheeks darken. "Only because he doesn't have an assistant."

She's wrong. Rhett and I haven't removed our clothes in his office. Not for lack of trying on his part. But I know better. The locks on the office doors are flimsy. Not to mention, all of the Raider brothers know how to pick locks and have no qualms about eavesdropping.

"Dakota!" Rhett motions me toward him.

Paisley grins as we walk toward the group of men. "This should be fun." She rubs her hands together. "What's the betting starting at?"

"The betting?"

She motions to the dartboards. "The betting for who wins."

I hold up my hands and retreat a few steps. "I'm not playing darts."

Kai slaps a set of darts into my hand. "If I have to play, so do you."

"What's wrong, little brother?" Zane asks. "Did the bartender not fall at your feet?"

Kai scowls. "Harper isn't the bartender. She's the owner."

While Miles and Zane tease Kai, I inch toward Rhett.

"I shouldn't be playing darts," I whisper to him.

He squeezes my shoulder. "There's no reason to be nervous. You're part of this family now."

As much as I want to enjoy his words, I can't. Not when I'm holding these death missiles in my hand.

"Jaxon doesn't have to play." I glance around. "He's your brother and he's not even here."

Rhett frowns. "Jaxon is an exception to every rule."

"But I—"

"Dakota!" Eli calls. "You're up first."

Rhett steers me toward the start line. He stands behind me and lifts my hand. "Grip the dart with three fingers. Let me show you." He loosens my grip. "Steady but not too tightly."

"Okay." I breathe out. I can do this. I can throw a dart and not injure anyone.

"Raise the dart to eye level and tilt the tip upward, aligning it with your target on the board."

Once I've followed his instructions, he steps away. "Now throw the dart with your hand and wrist, snapping your wrist as you…"

I miss the rest of what he's saying as I throw the dart. It flies into the air. But it's not heading in the direction of the board. It's aiming straight for Kai.

"Duck!" I yell.

Kai glances over his shoulder and – bam! – the dart hits him in the face. He grabs his nose as blood spurts out. I rush toward him but he waves me away.

"I believe there's a first aid kit behind the bar." He saunters toward the bar with a smirk on his face.

I stare after him. "Is he seriously using an injury to gain favor with a woman?"

Miles and Zane hurry after him. "Let's find out."

I shake my head and Rhett wraps an arm around my shoulders. "I don't think you have a future as a dart champion."

"I warned you."

He barks out a laugh. "I didn't think you'd try to take out Kai."

I huff. "I didn't try to take him out. If I wanted to take him out, he wouldn't be flirting with the owner."

"You're cute when you lie."

"I bet you say that to all the women."

"Nope." He kisses my nose. "There's only one woman I think is cute. One woman I want to spend my time with."

My heart thumps in my chest. Does he mean he…? He can't possibly. No. Rhett can't love me. I glance up at him from beneath my lashes. His blue eyes sparkle as he smiles at me.

Maybe he does love me. Maybe there is a happily ever after in my future after all.

Chapter 30

"Trick me once, I'm a fool. Trick me twice, and we're having words." ~ Rhett

RHETT

I stroll into the hallway at work and make my way to Dakota's desk. "What did the computer do to you?"

She scowls as she pounds on the keyboard. "Computer? Ha! Your brother is the one I wish I could pound."

I growl. "You won't be pounding my brother."

She freezes before glancing up at me. "I didn't mean pound as in…" Her cheeks darken. "As in the sexual variety. Gross. He's my boss."

I step closer. "But you enjoy bossy."

She rolls her eyes. "How many times do I have to explain bossy is not a compliment?"

"It's difficult to believe you when I know how much you enjoy me being bossy."

Her eyes flare. "I do not."

"Your squirming in your seat says otherwise."

"Shouldn't you be working?"

I bark out a laugh. "You can't change the subject of the discussion when you're losing."

She frowns. "You don't lose discussions. Discussions are not competitions."

"You obviously didn't grow up with five brothers."

Her chin drops and I swear. "I'm an asshole."

She blows out a breath before sitting up straight. "You're not an asshole. At least, not over this. I should be less sensitive. You shouldn't have to worry about what you say around me all the time."

I kneel before her and cup her face. "You can be as sensitive as you want, Havoc. You haven't had an easy life. I should be more considerate."

"I don't want you to have to worry about what you say."

I kiss her nose. "And I don't want you to be in pain, so we're even."

"Even?" She lifts a brow. "Everything's a contest to you, isn't it?"

She obviously doesn't want to discuss the deep stuff now. I let her get away with it. "And I'm winning."

"Of course, you are."

I stand. "You ready for lunch?"

Her eyes widen. "Lunch? It's lunchtime already?"

I indicate the clock. "Past lunch. It's already one."

"I didn't notice the time."

I offer her my hand. "Are you ready now?"

She slips her hand into mine and warmth spreads throughout my body. This must be how love feels. It's not only sweaty nights spent tangled in sheets. It's also the quiet contentedness of being around a person. Of wanting to spend all your time with that person.

She smiles up at me. "I'm ready."

I can't resist her smile. I need her taste on my tongue. I lean over and sip from her lips. The flavor of strawberry and sin fills me up. Since I've met Dakota, I can't look at a strawberry without getting hard.

I wrap my arms around her but she pushes me away.

"No sexy times at work."

I place my forehead against hers. "I have an office."

"And every single one of your brothers knows how to pick the lock to it."

"We can put a chair in front of the door."

She giggles. "You're incorrigible."

I'm hard as a rock, is what I am. This woman has no idea how sexy she is. How she drives me crazy.

"Fine. We'll have lunch at my house."

She lifts an eyebrow. "Because your brothers have never barged in on us there?"

I herd her toward the door and outside to my SUV.

"You better have food in your house," she says once we're driving.

I waggle my eyebrows at her. "I know something I can eat."

She slaps my shoulder. "Knock it off. I'm hungry."

Her stomach rumbles in agreement. "I can tell."

We arrive at my house a few minutes later. Dakota jumps out of the SUV before I can help her. I scowl.

"I told you I'm hungry. You shouldn't mess with a hungry woman."

"Lesson learned," I mutter as I open the door and motion her inside.

She aims straight for the kitchen. By the time I catch up with her, she has the refrigerator open and is pulling out cheese and cold cuts.

I stop her. "I can do this."

She startles. "Do you not want me rummaging around your refrigerator?"

I throw the food on the kitchen counter and slam the refrigerator shut before pressing her against it. "You can rummage around anywhere you want in my house. But you don't have to take care of me. I want to take care of you."

"I can take care of myself."

I tuck a strand of hair behind her ear. "I know. But you don't have to."

Her gaze meets mine and I get lost in those green eyes. They're full of wonder and a bit of fear. Damn. I don't want her to fear me. I want her to trust me. To know I won't screw her over the way her husband did.

I love her. She's mine to care for. I open my mouth to tell her as much but no words will come out.

An alarm beeps on her phone and she startles. "I need to deal with this."

She rushes off and relief pours through me. At lunchtime, while I have her pressed up against the refrigerator, is not the time to confess my love to Dakota. I should plan a romantic evening. She deserves flowers and chocolates, and romance.

As I prepare sandwiches for us, I consider the possibilities. A picnic on the beach or a candlelight dinner. Maybe I should make a reservation at *Hideaway Haven Resort.* The resort is on a secluded part of the island. I bet Dakota would enjoy it.

I frown when I realize she's been gone for five minutes. My brother should leave her alone during her lunchtime. She works hard enough for him. She deserves a break.

"Dakota," I holler but she doesn't reply.

I go in search of her. She's not in the living room or my office, as I expected. I knock on the powder room. "Havoc, are you in there?"

"Just a second!"

She sounds out of breath. "Are you okay?"

"I'm …" Something crashes to the floor.

I burst into the room. "What happened?"

My gaze lands on her. Her shirt is pulled up, and she's pressing a cotton swab to her stomach. "Did you hurt yourself?"

She bites her bottom lip. "Not exactly."

"Not exactly? What does …" I trail off when I notice the item on the vanity. A needle. There's a fucking needle on the vanity.

"Did you inject yourself?"

"Yes." She nods. "I—"

"You're using drugs in my house!" I grind my teeth. I can't believe this. Dakota is a drug user. "I fucking knew it!"

"Knew what?" she asks but I ignore her.

"I knew I couldn't trust you. I can't believe I ever thought I could. I can't believe I thought you were special." I shake my head. "Fooled again."

"You don't understand."

I cross my arms over my chest and glare at her. "Hell yea, I don't understand. I don't understand how you could lie to me. Lie to my face. I introduced you to my family. My brothers consider you their little sister. And all this time it's been a fucking lie."

Tears stream down her face. "It's not a lie. Let me explain."

"Explain how you're an addict? I don't think so."

"I'm not a—"

I slash a hand through the air. "Save it. I don't want to hear any more of your lies. I've heard enough."

"But—"

"In case I haven't made myself perfectly clear, we're over. I don't want to see your face ever again."

I slam the door and stomp to the front door. I'm in my vehicle, ready to pull out of the driveway, before I realize I can't leave a drug addict in my home alone.

"Damnit," I mutter as I make my way back inside.

Dakota is waiting for me in the foyer. Her eyes are swollen from her tears, and her mascara is smeared on her cheeks. Sympathy tries to push its way through my anger but I ignore it. She's an addict. And a liar. She doesn't deserve an ounce of sympathy from me.

"Thank you for coming back for me. Can I explain now?"

Heat flushes through my body as my anger flares. "I don't want an explanation."

"But—"

And I'm done. I can't listen to her try to wheedle her way back into my life while we drive to the distillery. I throw my keys at her. She fumbles them. I usually find it adorable when she's klutzy but now I have to wonder if it's an act. If everything she ever said and did was a lie.

"Go back to the distillery."

She opens her mouth to speak but I hold up a hand to stop her. "Leave the keys on my desk."

She stares at me for a moment before nodding. Her shoulders slump as she leaves my house and walks to the vehicle.

She can look as pathetic and upset as she wants. I'm not buying it. Because she's a liar.

Chapter 31

"Men suck. Female friends are awesome. That is all." ~ Dakota

DAKOTA

I don't know how I did it, but I made it through the work day. Rhett didn't return to the distillery, which helped.

I don't want to see his face. He couldn't have at least let me explain?

Relief fills me when I finally park at the *Mermaid Motel*. There's no way I'll run into Rhett here. He wouldn't deign to show his face at this motel if it weren't for me. Asshole.

The idea of working the night shift fills me with dread. I can't do it. Not tonight.

"Hey, Sadie," I greet as I walk into the reception area.

"What happened? Who do I need to banish from the island?"

I feign confusion. "What do you mean?"

She circles my face with her finger. "You've been crying."

Damnit. I scrubbed my face in the restroom at the distillery, but I guess I didn't do a good enough job.

"Can you cover for me tonight?"

"Of course."

Relief courses through me. I don't need to interact with other humans today. Thank the mermaids.

"If you tell me why you've been crying."

I groan. "There's always a catch with you."

"Duh." She rolls her eyes. "I'm a smuggler."

"I don't want to be a smuggler," I mutter.

"Now, I definitely know there's something wrong. You love this island."

I do. Smuggler's Hideaway is awesome. People are friendly, if a bit quirky. There's always some kind of festival going on. And I'm completely safe from my so-called friends who dumped me the minute they realized what a scoundrel Adam was.

Although, I'm not completely free from friends who've dumped me anymore.

"Rhett dumped me," I admit to Sadie.

"Shit." She rounds the counter to pull me into her arms. At first, I stiffen. I've never been the kind of woman who had friends who hug. But her arms around me feel good. I allow her to comfort me.

She leads me to the sofa in the reception area and pushes me down on it. "What happened?"

I fiddle with the strap of my purse. She squeezes my hand. "You can tell me. I won't tell anyone else."

I grab onto the chance to change the subject. "Really? Ms. Gossip All The Time won't spill the beans to the entire island?"

Her cheeks darken. "I can keep a secret."

"What secret are you keeping?"

"It wouldn't be a secret if I told you, would it?"

"But you admit there's a secret." I know there's a secret. There must be a reason she's super cagey about the mail.

"I admit to nothing." She taps my leg. "And you're stalling."

Of course, I'm stalling. I can't admit why Rhett dumped me without spilling my secrets. The door flies open before I can figure out how to explain what happened without revealing all. I frown when Blossom and Paisley rush inside.

"We came as soon as we could." Blossom hauls me to my feet and throws her arms around me. "We've got you," she murmurs as she sways me from side to side.

"How do you know?"

Blossom steps back and nods to Paisley.

"Sorry. But it's impossible to keep a secret in this family," Paisley says.

I scowl. Keeping secrets is what got me into this mess in the first place.

The door opens again and a group of college kids stroll inside. Sadie makes her way to the desk. "I'll cover you for tonight, but I expect answers later."

Blossom and Paisley usher me toward the door. When they start to push me toward the parking lot, I plant my feet.

"No way. I'm not leaving." I'm not chancing running into Rhett. I don't want him to know how devastated I am. How heartbroken I am.

He's an asshole. He doesn't deserve to witness my pain.

Blossom threads her arm through mine. "I suspected as much."

We make our way to my suite. Paisley's lips flatten as she scans the living area. "Eli doesn't pay you enough."

Eli pays me just fine. But she won't be hearing from me why I'm living in this crummy owner's suite.

"I have moonshine or beer. Your choice." Blossom holds up a bottle of beer in one hand and a bottle of moonshine in the other.

"I don't drink."

Paisley nods. "A good decision considering your condition."

Blossom drops the bottles onto the kitchen counter with a gasp. "You're pregnant? Rhett dumped you when you're pregnant? I'm going to kill him. He can join Jaxon at the bottom of a nameless grave."

"Whoa. No killing necessary. I'm not pregnant."

Blossom's brow furrows. "Then, what condition is Paisley referring to?"

"She has diabetes."

I glare at Paisley. "How do you know?"

She shrugs. "It's obvious. You always carry hard candy and juice boxes with you. You don't drink. And I've noticed a bandage on your finger a few times." She clears her throat and pushes her glasses up her nose. "The question I have is, why do you keep your disease a secret. It's nothing to be ashamed of."

Easy for her to say. She wasn't rejected time and time again for adoption. She doesn't know how it feels to have a couple claim to want to adopt you and then change their minds once they learn your mother was a drug addict.

"I don't care why you kept it secret." Blossom pushes a glass of juice into my hands. "I care why Rhett dumped you because you have diabetes. What a jerk! He's worse than his brother."

Paisley purses her lips. "Eli is a good man."

Blossom waves away her objection. "I wasn't speaking about Eli."

"Ah, yes." Paisley nods. "Your 'agreement' with Jaxon."

Blossom scowls. "There's no agreement with Jaxon."

Paisley snorts. "And Dakota isn't heartbroken about Rhett either."

They turn toward me and I hold up my hands. Juice spills over the side of the glass and splashes on my top. "Ugh. Klutzy Dakota strikes again."

Blossom throws a towel at me, and Paisley snatches my juice away.

"Don't think you're getting out of this conversation by spilling on yourself," Blossom says as I blot my blouse with the towel.

My shoulders fall. "What do you want to know?"

She sits next to me on the sofa and grasps my hand. "Why didn't you tell Rhett? You love him. You shouldn't keep secrets from each other."

"You make it sound easy."

Paisley barks out a laugh. "Falling in love isn't easy. I watched all of my friends fall in love and thought it was the easiest thing ever. But it's not."

I sigh. "I don't know. Falling in love with Rhett was pretty easy. I thought after…" I shake my head. I've never told my friends about my dead husband.

"After what?" Blossom pushes.

"I'm a horrible friend."

Paisley's brow wrinkles. "How did we go from you telling us about loving Rhett to you being a horrible friend?"

"I've been keeping secrets from you. Friends don't keep secrets from each other."

Blossom shrugs. "There's a difference between keeping secrets and things you haven't told us yet because you're always working and we haven't known you long."

"I like your point of view."

"You should. I'm always right."

I giggle. I nearly startle at the sound. I didn't think I'd ever giggle again after what happened today.

"Tell us. What's this big secret you're keeping?"

"Well," I begin, before telling them all about my dead husband.

"Phew!" Blossom runs the back of her hand over her forehead in a dramatic gesture once I've finished. "I was worried you were going to say you're leaving Smuggler's Hideaway."

I actually hadn't considered leaving the island. Where would I go? It's difficult enough to find one job but find two? I'm lucky to have the jobs I have.

"Why would she leave the island?" Paisley asks. "It's awesome here."

"And she has awesome friends here." Blossom winks.

"And a good job."

I groan. "A good job where I have to run into the ex I'm in love with every day."

Blossom waves away my concern. "No need to worry. The Raider brothers are exceptional at avoiding women when they want to."

"I guess I'm staying on Smuggler's Hideaway."

"Yea!" Blossom cheers.

"I think we should brainstorm some pranks we can pull on Rhett," Paisley adds.

"You're a dark horse. You appear all nerdy with your glasses and obsession with chemistry and then bam! You coat Eli's office with red dye."

"Trust me. He deserved it."

"What did he do?" Blossom leans close to ask.

As Paisley tells the story of what a jerk Eli was, I sit back and enjoy myself.

I thought I'd found a family on Smuggler's Hideaway. And I did. It's just not the family I thought it was. Instead of Rhett's family becoming mine. I created my own family. One I can rely on when my life goes to shit.

I thought my friends abandoned me when Adam's secrets came out. I was wrong. Those women weren't my friends.

I smile at Paisley and Blossom. These women are.

I'm going to be okay. Just as soon as Paisley explains how I can make red dye explode all over Rhett the asshole's office.

Chapter 32

*"Can I exchange my brothers for new ones?" ~
Rhett*

RHETT

I slide the drawer closed but it gets stuck. I push harder until it slams into place with a whack. I mutter a few choice swear words under my breath.

Zane skips into my office. "Uh oh. Mr. Bossypants is in a bad mood."

"I thought we agreed to call him Mr. High and Mighty," Miles says as he strolls inside.

I scowl at them. "What do you want?"

Zane taps his chin. "Maybe we should call him grumpy pants."

Miles smiles. "I approve."

"Shouldn't you be surfing?"

"He's not merely grumpy, he's also blind." Miles motions to the window behind me. "Even I can't surf in this weather."

Zane elbows him. "Admit it. You want to try."

"I'm not visiting you in the hospital when you wipe out," I say.

"Asshole," Miles mutters before fleeing.

"Dude." Zane shakes his head. "You can be grumpy but there's no reason to bring up Miles's accident."

Fuck. Miles is very sensitive about the accident that caused him to give up his dream of becoming a professional surfer. I rub a hand down my face. "I didn't mean to bring up his accident."

Kai peeks into my office. "Where's the fire?"

"There's no fire."

"Then, why was I told to report to your office pronto?"

I blow out a breath. "Because it's apparently torture Rhett time."

"Nah, dude," Zane says. "We're trying to cheer you up."

I don't bother asking why they feel the need to cheer me up. It's not exactly a secret that I dumped Dakota.

"By calling me grumpy?"

He shrugs. "I didn't say the plan was perfect."

"I got this." Kai rubs his hands together. "Brother, you remind me of a country song – you just need a truck, a lost dog, and a bottle of whiskey."

Zane snickers. "Good thing we own a distillery."

"Do we need to call a doctor?" Kai asks. "Because this level of pathetic might be a medical condition."

I growl at him. "I'm not pathetic."

"But you are broken," Zane says.

"I haven't seen something this broken since Mom's favorite vase 'mysteriously' fell off the shelf," Kai adds.

Zane throws his hands in the air. "It wasn't my fault."

It was totally his fault. Baseball is not an indoor sport, no matter what my brother thinks.

"I'd say there are 'plenty of fish in the sea,' but let's be real – you ain't exactly a skilled fisherman."

I glare at Kai. "I know how to fish."

Zane shakes his head. "Dude."

"What's going on?" Eli asks as he enters my office.

Finally. A responsible brother. "These two are just leaving to get back to work."

"Boring," Kai mutters. "No wonder Dakota dumped him."

Zane studies me. "Do you think he's boring in bed?"

"I am not boring in bed," I grumble.

"Let's ask Dakota." Kai starts for the door.

"Don't you dare bother her."

"Because you care for her?" Kai asks.

"Or because you know she'll confirm you're boring in bed?" Zane asks.

"Whatever." I throw my hands in the air. "You stay here. I'll go work in Kai's office."

Kai's eyes widen. "I have an office?"

"I blame you," I tell Eli.

"Me?" He taps his chest. "What did I do?"

"You're the one who thought it would be a good idea to found a company with the Raider brothers."

Kai smiles. "It was an excellent idea."

"Totally excellent." Zane and Kai high-five each other.

"Enough shenanigans," Eli declares. "Everyone out."

I'm not going anywhere. "This is my office."

Eli rolls his eyes. "Except you. We need to talk."

Kai pats Eli's shoulder. "Good luck with the grumpy one."

Eli pushes Kai and Zane out of the room and shuts the door behind them. I collapse in my chair. "They're just going to eavesdrop from Zane's office."

Eli sits across from me and grins. "But we can pretend we don't hear them."

"No one puts baby in the corner," Kai shouts.

"I got this," Eli mutters as he pulls his phone out of his pocket and starts typing. "That should do it," he says before pushing send and stuffing his phone back in his pocket.

Barely five seconds pass before I hear a stampede in the hallway. "What did you do?"

He shrugs. "I said I'd pay their bar tab today."

I whistle. "It's barely noon. That's going to be some bar tab."

"What's the sense of being a billionaire if I can't pay a bar tab for my brothers once in a while?"

"Don't expect me to watch over them. I have work to do."

"I don't expect you to watch over them."

"You're on the hook for bail money."

"I opened an account with the police department a while back."

I lean back in my chair. "What did you need to discuss?"

Eli lifts a brow. "You have to ask?"

"Shit," I mutter. I had hoped my big brother was here about work. I hate to be wrong, especially when it means I have to discuss my failures.

"What happened?"

I scratch my chin. "With?"

"Seriously? My personal assistant has been crying her eyes out all morning. What happened?"

I frown as guilt stabs me. I ignore it. I don't have a reason to feel guilty. I'm not the one who was keeping secrets. I'm not the one who tricked someone into falling in love with me. I'm not the liar.

"Crap." Eli sighs. "I don't want to fire Dakota. She's a damn fine assistant but judging by the way you're grinding your teeth there's no way the two of you can work together."

Panic lashes at me. Dakota may be a liar. But her desperation for money is real. Her late husband screwed her over bad.

"You can't fire Dakota."

"Pretty sure I can."

"No, Eli. I'm serious. You can't fire her."

"But you two can't work together anymore. I knew I should have forbidden you from dating her. But you always kept your distance from the women you dated before. I assumed you'd have a fling and be over it. I didn't think I'd find my assistant crying in the bathroom."

Fuck. Dakota was crying in the bathroom.

"And you trying to break your desk."

I jump at the chance to keep the conversation focused on me. I can't think about Dakota crying in the bathroom. Her tears kill me. "I didn't try to break my desk."

"Jaxon heard you in the distillery."

"Liar. The distillery could burn down around him and he wouldn't notice."

"I heard you."

"I just need some time. I should have worked at home, but I needed to pick up some documents, and the phone rang, and before I knew it, I'd been here all morning."

"What happened?"

"I don't want to discuss it."

"Too bad."

"It's none of your business."

"Wrong. You dated my assistant. I need to know if I should fire her."

"Our breakup had nothing to do with her work here."

"If she broke your heart, I'll fire her."

I rub a hand over my chest. "You can't fire her for breaking my heart."

He smirks. "You admitted she broke your heart."

"Asshole," I mutter.

He shrugs. "I wouldn't need to be an asshole if you'd just come out and tell me what happened."

"You're not going to give up, are you?"

"Nope."

"Why don't you ask Dakota? She works for you. She's required to answer you."

"You work for me. You're required to answer me."

I shake my head. "She wouldn't tell you, would she?"

"The woman is Fort Knox."

"I'd be Fort Knox if I was a drug addict, too," I mutter.

"What?" He explodes. "My assistant is an addict?" He jumps to his feet. "That's cause for immediate termination." He begins to pace the room. "I'll need you to write a witness account. I don't want her suing me."

"Easy enough. I saw her injecting herself in the stomach in my hall powder room."

He freezes. "In the stomach?"

I nod.

"And you didn't find this odd?"

"I wasn't concerned with the location. I was more concerned with the needle."

He collapses in a chair. "She didn't tell you. She told me she didn't want anyone knowing, but I figured she told you."

"You knew?" My jaw aches from how hard I'm grinding my teeth and I force myself to stop. I can't believe this. Eli fucking knew I was dating a drug addict and didn't tell me. What the actual hell?

"Listen." He clears his throat. "I think there's been a misunderstanding."

"A misunderstanding?"

"Dakota isn't a drug addict. She's a diabetic."

My whole world spins on its axis. Dakota is a diabetic. I can't believe this.

"A diabetic? But how? And why didn't she tell me?"

He shrugs. "I don't know but guessing by your reaction to seeing a needle, she might have been afraid of your reaction."

"No." I shake my head. "Don't blame this on me."

He holds up his hands. "I'm not blaming anyone. I'm merely pointing out that had you asked Dakota for an explanation, she could have explained she's not an addict."

"I did ask her…" I snap my mouth closed when I remember I didn't ask her for an explanation. In fact, when she tried to explain, I wouldn't let her. Am I the asshole?

Eli pushes to his feet. "I'm glad we resolved this."

"We didn't resolve shit."

"Sure, we did. You're an asshole. Dakota isn't an addict. Problem solved."

"How is the problem solved?" As far as I can tell, the problem is worse than when he arrived. It's a big pile of shit I not only stepped into. I also stomped around in it before dragging shit everywhere.

"I assume you're going to grovel for forgiveness since you jumped to conclusions," he says as he leaves.

Is Eli right? Should I grovel for forgiveness? Did I jump to conclusions?

My heart spasms in my chest. Dakota isn't a drug addict. She could be mine if I apologize.

Is that what I want?

Chapter 33

"Now I understand why so many jokes are made about work. Work sucks." ~ Dakota

DAKOTA

I park my car in front of the distillery and blow out a breath. I can do this. There are more difficult things than working with Rhett the Asshole all day. Lord knows I've been through worse.

My heart spasms. It doesn't agree. For reasons I don't care to think about for too long, Rhett dumping me hurts worse than finding out my husband was a lying, cheating scumbag wanker.

I check my eyes in the rearview mirror. My eyes aren't too puffy, are they? I hope not.

The last thing I need is my boss, Eli, to try and comfort me in the restroom when I've been crying. The man is not good at pep talks. Although when he growled about killing his brother, I nearly cheered.

I notice the time on the clock. Shit. I'm going to be late. I don't need to give Eli any more excuses to fire me. I need this job. Health insurance is worth it, I remind myself as I climb out of my car.

"Hey, Dakota!" Miles waves at me as he hurries across the parking lot toward me.

I nearly cringe at his use of my real name. None of Rhett's brothers have called me anything other than 'little sis' since Rhett and I started dating.

"What are you doing here this early? Did you break your surfboard?" I tease instead of breaking down into tears about how the Raiders were never really my family.

"Hit the waves at dawn this morning. Dawn patrol is the best."

"Huh. Maybe you could surf early every morning and come to work on time?"

He scowls at me. "Sounds boring."

"Welcome to adulting."

"Nah." He smirks. "I don't adult."

"Must be nice," I mutter.

Resentment rears its ugly head. It would be nice to have a billionaire brother who founded a company just so you could have a job. A job you can ignore as much as you want because your brother is never going to fire you.

"Hey." Miles squeezes my shoulder. "I was joking."

I force a smile. I'm not going to be a bitch to him. He's not the brother I have a problem with. It's not his fault I fell in love with his asshole brother.

"I know. It's all good."

He frowns. "I don't know much about women."

I snort. "Really?" Look up charming in the dictionary and you'll find a picture of Miles.

"Let me rephrase. I don't understand much about women. But I figure *It's all good* is similar to *It's fine* which every man worth his weight in sea salt means nothing is fine."

I don't want to discuss how nothing in my life is fine. How I have no choice but to continue to work in the same office mere feet from the man who broke my heart.

I hold up a hand. "Watch it, charming surfer dude. You're awful close to adulting right now."

He feigns retching. "Thanks for the warning, Dakota." He unlocks the door before sauntering away to his office.

I wish I had an office. I could hide in there all day. Hiding in the restroom is out since Eli has no problem barging in to check on me. I had to find the one billionaire boss who understands the word sympathy.

I switch on the lights as I make my way to my desk. I frown when I notice my desk isn't empty. I always make sure my desk is cleared off at the end of the work day. There's nothing worse than a cluttered desk.

Hold on. It's a gift basket. Announce to the world how you found me crying in the bathroom, why don't you, Eli?

I snatch the card and read it. *Sorry, I overreacted.*

Damnit. There's only one person who overreacted and he's not supposed to know why he overreacted since he didn't let me explain.

I grab the basket – intent on setting it somewhere out of sight – but curiosity gets the best of me. I unpack it instead.

Glucose tablets, nuts, protein bars, a compact first-aid kit with alcohol wipes and a backup syringe, band-aids, sugar-free chocolates, and a candy jar filled with jellybeans. The pink ribbon around the jar reads *Break in case of low blood sugar or when you need a little extra sweetness.*

"Do you like it?"

I screech and clasp my chest before whirling around to confront Rhett. "You scared the mermaid out of me."

He scratches his chin. "Sorry. I thought you heard me."

"You should wear a bell."

"And let my brothers know I'm coming?" He shakes his head.

I roll my eyes. "You wouldn't want to lose the prank war."

He motions to the gift basket. "Do you like it?"

I love it. Most people do not react to finding out I'm a diabetic by giving me a gift basket. Usually, they run the other way. Or break up with me.

"I guess you figured out I'm not a drug addict."

He grimaces. "I should have let you explain."

Damn right, he should have. But he didn't, so how did he find out?

"Who told you?"

"Eli."

I should have known. He's the only person who knows about my illness. Except my friends who I trust not to blabber to Rhett. Especially since they've nicknamed him the Dodge Master.

"Eli's got a big mouth."

"Eli cares about you."

I snort. "Because no other assistant would answer their phone at four o'clock in the morning."

He scowls. "Eli calls you at four in the morning?"

"It's fine. I'm awake at my other job anyway."

"I hate you having two jobs."

Who does he think he is? Mr. High and Mighty is not allowed to comment on my life. Not anymore.

"Good thing your opinion on how many jobs I have is irrelevant. In fact, your opinion on anything I do is completely irrelevant since we're no longer involved."

He rears back. "I apologized."

I fist my hands on my hips. "You did?"

He steps toward me but I back up. I can't allow him too close to me. If he is, I'll probably do something stupid like throw myself at him. Bad idea. The man broke my heart at the first hurdle in our relationship.

I deserve more. I deserve a man who thinks I hung the moon. Who doesn't assume the worst in me the second he sees something he doesn't understand.

"I'm sorry, Dakota. I overreacted. I should have let you explain. I shouldn't have broken us apart."

I try to hang onto my anger. But try as I might, I can't. Not when Rhett's staring at me with those piercing blue eyes, looking as chagrined as a boy who got caught with his hand in the cookie jar.

Miles may not be able to adult, but I can. "I accept your apology."

Rhett's eyes warm and he sighs. "Thank fuck."

He reaches for me but I hold up a hand. "I accept your apology, but it doesn't change anything."

His brow wrinkles. "What do you mean?"

I motion between us. "This doesn't work."

"I recall us working pretty damn well."

Sparks ignite in my belly at the heat in his eyes. I ignore it. Good sex is not enough to keep a relationship together.

"I'm not referring to our sexual chemistry."

He clears his throat. "There's more to us than our sexual chemistry."

I wave toward the gift basket. "And yet you didn't trust me enough to let me explain myself when you caught me injecting myself with insulin."

He winces. "And I'm going to regret my actions for the rest of my life."

"There's no reason to be full of regret. Let's learn from our mistakes and move on."

"I can't move on, Havoc."

"I'm sorry, Rhett. But I can't be with a man who lashes out at me the way you did. You dumped me and broke my heart for nothing."

A muscle in his jaw ticks. "It was a misunderstanding."

"It didn't need to be."

"Can I explain why I overreacted?"

I nearly tell him no. What good will knowing the reason behind his actions do? It won't change anything. But I can't resist his pleading face. I'm such a sucker.

"Go ahead."

He glances around the room. "Not here. Where my brothers are eavesdropping on us."

"Hey!" Miles shouts. "Not fair. I'm the only brother in the office."

Rhett growls. "Go away, Miles!"

"Not until you grovel to Dakota and make her our little sister again."

Heat radiates through my chest, and my hands tingle. I want that. I want to be part of a family. Someone's little sister.

"I can't grovel while you're eavesdropping!" Rhett shouts back and I giggle. I can't help myself. Rhett and his brothers are utterly ridiculous.

"She laughed. You're good!" Miles shouts.

"I'm still waiting for an explanation," I holler at him but he doesn't respond.

"I'll give you an explanation tonight," Rhett says. "I promise."

I blow out a breath. "Fine. We can use the conference room after all your brothers have left."

"Nope. I'm taking you out for dinner at the resort."

"The resort?" *Hideaway Haven Resort* is the only resort on Smuggler's Hideaway. It's also super expensive since its clientele are the rich and famous.

"Yep. I'll pick you up at the motel at seven." He saunters away before I have a chance to protest.

My muscles vibrate with excitement as I watch him leave. I try to calm them down but I can't. Rhett is taking me to a fancy restaurant.

To apologize, I remind myself. And he's my ex.

But he doesn't want to be.

Nope. I'm not thinking about this. It's time to work.

Chapter 34

"I am not letting Dakota slip away from me. She wants to run away. I'm chasing her." ~ Rhett

RHETT

Excitement vibrates through my body as I pull into the *Mermaid Motel* parking lot. Dakota hasn't forgiven me yet, but she will. I won't settle for anything less. Because Dakota is mine. She's the woman I love. The woman I plan to spend the rest of my days with.

I stop in front of her suite and her door opens. I jump out of my vehicle.

"You were supposed to wait for me to knock."

She rolls her eyes. "Mr. High and Mighty has arrived at the party."

I start to tell her I'm not high or mighty but my words get caught in my throat when I notice what she's wearing. The black dress hugs all her curves. My mouth waters. I want my hands on those curves again while she's writhing beneath me in passion. My cock twitches. It's on board.

"What's wrong?" she asks and I realize I'm standing still in the parking lot staring at her. I hope I'm not drooling.

I clear my throat. "I want to throw you over my shoulder and drag you into the hotel room and do dirty, dirty things to you."

Her cheeks warm and the flush travels down her neck to her chest. I groan at the peek of her breasts.

"Sorry," she breathes out. "No bedroom shenanigans."

I'll change her mind. I'll confess why I was a complete dumbass and get her to forgive me. I won't – can't – accept any other alternative.

I open the door to my SUV and help her inside. I can't resist trailing my fingers over her hips as I lift her. Her breath hitches and I duck my head to hide my smile. Dakota still wants me. She just doesn't want to.

"How's your blood sugar?" I ask once I'm driving toward the *Hideaway Haven Resort.*

She frowns at me. "I've been handling my diabetes by myself for a long time. I don't need you to control me."

"I'm not trying to control you. I'm concerned. Diabetes isn't a joke."

"You're telling me," she mumbles.

"I'm sorry you have to deal with this. It can't be easy."

"It's fine."

I may have been an idiot before but I can recognize when a woman is done with a conversation. We fall into silence. I can feel the nervous energy emitting from her. She's not the only one who's nervous. Tonight's conversation is the most important one of my life. I can't fuck it up.

Good thing the trip to the resort isn't long, since the tension in the vehicle grows as I drive. By the time I park, I'm biting my tongue to stop myself from blurting out how much I love her and what an idiot I am.

"Wait for me," I insist.

"I'm waiting but not because you ordered me to." I lift an eyebrow. She motions to her dress. "I'm afraid I'll get arrested for indecent exposure if I try to climb out of your oversized SUV without help."

"Don't be silly." I smirk. "No one gets arrested for indecent exposure on the island."

I jump out and round the vehicle to open her door.

"They don't?"

I have to fight to remember what we were discussing. With my hands on her body, my mind goes blank. I set her down and clear my throat.

"Ask Miles some time about how he decided to surf in the nude."

She giggles. "Why am I not surprised?"

I offer her my arm, and to my relief, she takes it. We walk into the restaurant and she gasps.

"Holy smugglers in hell. This is fancy."

Did I screw up? Is it too fancy? Is she intimidated? Does she not like the place?

I glance down at her and her green eyes are wide with wonder. I blow out a breath. I need to stop second guessing myself. Everything is going to work out. It has to. I love her.

The host shows us to our table. It's in an alcove with views of the ocean.

Dakota opens her menu and lifts it in front of her face. Oh no, she doesn't. She's not hiding from me. Not tonight. I snatch the menu from her.

"Hey!"

"I need to explain why I was an asshole when I caught you…" I wave my hand. "You know."

"Injecting myself with insulin," she supplies.

I nod. "Yes, injecting yourself with insulin."

"What I don't understand is how you jumped to the conclusion that I'm a drug addict? Wouldn't there have been other signs I'm an addict?"

I frown. This is the perfect lead-in to explain why I reacted the way I did. I hate to admit my faults but here we are.

"I didn't see the signs before."

Her brow wrinkles. "You've dated a drug addict before?"

"No. Not a drug addict." I inhale a deep breath and dive in. "I didn't see the signs before when someone lied to me and misled me." She gasps but I keep going. "I've had a hard time trusting anyone since then."

"Thus, Mr. Controlling."

I nod. "Exactly. If I'm in control, people won't let me down."

She reaches across the table to clasp my hand. "Who let you down?"

"My dad."

Her brow furrows. "I remember you said your dad left."

"There's more to the story."

She squeezes my hand. "What happened?"

"I hate discussing this."

"Okay."

I blow out a breath of relief. She's letting me off the hook. But then I realize she's standing. "Where are you going?"

"If you aren't going to explain why you..." She clears her throat. "...you know. Then, there's no reason for us to have dinner together."

I growl. There's every reason for us to have dinner together. This is the first of many dinners together. But first...

"I said I hate discussing this. I didn't say I wouldn't."

She sits back down. "Please, proceed."

"My dad left us when I was fifteen."

"I'm sorry."

I wave away her apology. "He's an asshole for leaving us but my problem isn't *that* he left us it's *how* he left." I pause to gather my courage. "He planned everything in advance. He had a woman waiting for him in another apartment in another city in another state, and we knew nothing. He said he loved us, kissed my mom goodbye, and left for a business meeting. He never returned. Hell, he dropped all contact with us."

"You didn't see the signs then and now you're terrified you'll miss the signs when someone is lying to you?"

I nod. "Now do you understand why I overreacted?"

"I do." Dakota smiles, but sadness fills her eyes. "Three couples. Three times I thought I was going to be adopted. Three times the couples rejected me after they found out about my medical and health issues."

"Fuck," I mutter. "Assholes."

She holds up a hand. "I don't blame them. I understand. A child with a chronic illness is a lot to take on. But the experiences taught me to keep my health problems to myself."

Pain slices through me. How can I blame her for keeping her diabetes a secret, considering her past? I should have been more considerate. I should have listened to her.

"I'm sorry. I'm sorry I didn't trust you. I'm sorry my abandonment issues reared their ugly head and I hurt you." I reach across the table to grasp her hands. "Can you ever forgive me?"

"Can you forgive me for not trusting you enough to tell you about my diabetes?"

"It's forgotten. I should have handled the woman I love with more care."

Her mouth gapes open. "The woman you love?"

I grin. "I love you, Dakota. You came into my life and wreaked havoc. You broke down all my walls. I was determined to never fall in love. To never find a wife. Because I knew there wasn't a woman out there I could trust. I was wrong."

Her eyes well with tears.

"Don't cry. Please, don't cry. Your tears slay me."

"It's your fault." Her voice wobbles as the tears break free. "You're being sweet."

I stand and haul her into my arms. "Get used to it, Havoc. I love you."

She glances up at me. Her green eyes are full of wonder. "I love you, too."

"Thank fuck," I mutter before molding my lips to hers. I groan as her taste hits me. It's only been a few days since I've touched her, but those days felt like they lasted years. Not knowing if I would ever feel her again. Wondering how I would survive without her.

"Hey!"

I startle at the shout and pull away from Dakota to glare at my brother. Unfortunately, Kai isn't alone. All of my brothers and Dakota's friends are here.

"What's going on?" Dakota asks.

Blossom throws her arms in the air. "We're here to celebrate your relationship!"

Jaxon flinches and she glares at him. "Excuse me. I'm so sorry if it's impossible for you to pretend I don't exist when I shout."

"I'm not pretending you don't exist."

Blossom snorts. "Liar. Liar. Pants on fire."

Jaxon lifts his glasses and pinches his nose. "I'm not a liar."

"Seriously? You walked into a wall to avoid me."

Paisley glances back and forth between the two. "I'm confused. I thought you two were hooking up at the distillery."

Jaxon's face blushes until it's bright enough to be used as a lighthouse. "It was a mistake."

"A mistake?" Blossom screeches. "I'm a mistake?"

She marches off and Jaxon stares after her. Miles pushes him. "Go after her."

Jaxon frowns at Miles before following Blossom out of the restaurant.

I throw an arm around Dakota's shoulders and draw her near. "Are you ready to join my crazy family?"

"I love your family." I scowl and she kisses my nose. "But not as much as I love you."

"Good. Since you are never getting rid of me."

"Same, Mr. High and Mighty. Same."

Chapter 35

BLOSSOM

I glance at the clock. Thirty minutes. I have less than half an hour to finish this inventory, order any missing supplies, and get changed for the party. I can do this.

Ha! I throw my arms in the air in celebration when I finish ordering the supplies in less than twenty minutes. Ten minutes to change. More than I need.

There's a knock on the restroom door when I'm applying my lipstick. "Blossom, are you ready?"

I open the door and flash a smile at my boss, Paisley. "With five minutes to spare."

"Your obsession with time management rivals mine."

"There's a reason you hired me."

We walk out of the brewery to my car. I'm giving her a ride since her boyfriend, Eli, will be at the restaurant and will drive her home.

"I hope everything works out," I say as I drive toward the restaurant.

"Rhett is a Raider. He'll convince Dakota to give him another chance."

I smirk at her. "You sound experienced."

"Eli is very persuasive."

My stomach cramps but I ignore it. I'm happy for my friends. I am. Paisley and Dakota deserve all the happiness in the world. It's not their fault I'm obsessed with a Raider brother who pretends I don't exist.

Except for the time Jaxon and I made out at the distillery. I nearly fan myself. His kisses turned me on like no man before him has done. Unfortunately for me, Jaxon said it was a mistake and has been ignoring me since. And, trust me, I've done everything I can think of to get his attention.

We arrive at *Hideaway Haven Resort* and make our way to the restaurant. I frown when I notice the Raider brothers are waiting in the hallway.

"What's going on?" I ask as we approach.

Eli points inside. "Rhett is still groveling."

Miles chuckles. "It's hilarious."

"We should have planted a microphone at their table," Zane says.

Kai sighs. "I tried. The hostess wouldn't take a bribe."

Only one Raider brother doesn't speak – Jaxon. He fiddles with his glasses. Why are his nerdy tendencies sexy? Since when am I into nerds?

Saying Jaxon is a nerd isn't an exaggeration – he's the smartest person I know, obsessed with distilling the best whiskey ever made, and lacks social skills – but, except for the glasses, he doesn't resemble a classic nerd.

He's tall with broad shoulders. I've never met a nerd with the muscles Jaxon has. I've had the chance to touch his spectacular shoulders and biceps once before but guessing by the way his t-shirt strains over his chest, those pec muscles are spectacular, too.

And he has those classic Raider blue eyes. They pierce through you. When the man deigns to meet your gaze, which, if your name is Blossom, doesn't occur often.

Finally, his jaw is covered with scruff since he always forgets to shave. Fine by me. I love running my fingernails over a beard.

"Uh oh," Miles mutters and I shake my head to force my Jaxon cloud away. "Dakota's crying."

"Those are happy tears," Paisley says.

"How can you tell?" Zane pushes his way to the front. "Oh."

"Oh, what?" I elbow my way through the brothers. "Ah," I say when I catch the couple making out.

Kai smirks. "Time to interrupt." He marches through the hotel with Miles and Zane hot on his heels.

I chase after them. "Can't you let them kiss for a while?"

"Where's the fun in that?" Zane asks.

He has a point.

"Hey!" Kai shouts as we reach their table and they startle apart.

"What's going on?" Dakota asks.

I throw my arms in the air. "We're here to celebrate your relationship!"

Jaxon flinches, and I glare at him. "Excuse me. I'm so sorry it's impossible for you to pretend I don't exist when I shout."

"I'm not pretending you don't exist."

I snort. "Liar. Liar. Pants on fire."

Jaxon lifts his glasses and pinches his nose. I refuse to find the gesture adorable. Re-fuse! "I'm not a liar."

"Seriously? You walked into a wall to avoid me."

Paisley glances back and forth between us. "I'm confused. I thought you two were hooking up in the distillery."

She saw us? She never mentioned a thing. We work together every day. And we're friends.

A blush covers Jaxon's face. "It was a mistake."

"A mistake?" I screech. "I'm a mistake?"

I'll put up with a lot of shit from a man. As evidenced by my asshole ex who I should have left long before he cheated on me. But saying I'm a mistake? No way. Nuh huh. I have more pride than to be referred to as a mistake.

I spin around and march out of the restaurant. I do not want to breathe the same air as Jaxon right now. He can fall off of a cliff for all I care. Would it be wrong if I pushed him? Probably. Stupid morals.

"Blossom!" Jaxon shouts.

I glance behind me to find him chasing me. Now, he chases me? When we're in a crowded resort with all of his family watching?

Two can play at his hide and seek game. I scan the hallway I'm running down. There. An open door.

I rush inside and slam the door shut behind me. Jaxon will never find me now.

"Blossom?"

Mother fluffing ducks not in a row. Speaking of exes. I close my eyes and hope I'm hallucinating due to lack of oxygen. I really should work out more.

"Is that you, Blossom?"

Damn. No such luck. I force a smile on my face and spin around.

"Alan. What are you doing here?"

He chuckles. "I was about to ask you the same thing."

"I live on Smuggler's Hideaway." My cheeks are starting to hurt from how hard I'm forcing this fake smile.

"I always wondered where you ended up."

"Welp. Here I am." I throw my arms in the air. "What are you doing here?"

I cross my fingers behind my back. *Please don't say you're moving here. Please don't say you're moving here.* Talk about a disaster in the making.

Alan grins. "I'm getting married here."

"Here? As in on the island of Smuggler's Hideaway?"

He nods. "In this resort."

Bleeping smugglers drowning in the sea. Thanks for the reminder that things can always get worse.

"Congratulations! Where's your future wife?" I scan the room, which I now realize is filled with all things bridal – sample bouquets, various champagnes, a plethora of cakes, etc.

"Stacey hasn't arrived yet."

At least he's not marrying the tramp he cheated on me with. I don't care who he's marrying. I need to extract myself from this conversation and leave.

"Too bad. I would have loved to meet her." This is my cue to exit.

"You can meet her. Why don't you come to the wedding?"

I snap my mouth shut before my jaw drops to the floor. Why the hell would I want to come to his wedding?

"And I can meet your husband," he continues.

Well, shit.

"There is a husband, isn't there?"

I know it's wrong to lie, but I had my reasons for lying. And they were good. But a lie is a lie.

"Of course, there is."

There's a knock on the door. "Blossom, are you in there?"

"There he is now."

I open the door and haul Jaxon to me. "Look who I ran into, honey bunches of oats."

"Um…"

I widen my eyes in a plea for his help.

"How would I know who you ran into? You were hiding from me."

I force out a giggle. "Because I enjoy it when you chase me."

Alan steps forward and offers Jaxon his hand. "I'm Alan."

"Jaxon." They shake. Jaxon looks adorably confused while Alan appears annoyed.

"You don't know who I am?" Alan asks.

"Should I?"

"I'm Alan," my ex announces as if he's a superstar. He always did have delusions of grandeur.

"Yes, you said."

I sputter out a laugh and Alan glares at me. "Sorry. Jaxon isn't very good with names."

Alan narrows his eyes on Jaxon as he studies him. "But I'm your ex. Your husband should know your ex-boyfriend's name."

Jaxon's eyes widen. Before he can open his mouth and prove I'm a liar, Terri, the event coordinator for the resort, sweeps into the room.

"I'm sorry." She lays some lacy material over the table. "I think this is the color you want."

I grasp Jaxon's hand and back out of the room. "We'll leave you to your preparations."

"I'll see you next weekend," Alan calls as I flee the room.

"Next weekend?" Jaxon asks as I drag him away.

I glance around to ensure no one's eavesdropping before answering. "At his wedding."

Jaxon skids to a stop. "His wedding?"

I gulp. "He kind of invited us."

"Us? Why would he invite us?" Understanding lights his blue eyes. "Because he believes we're married. Why did you tell him we're married?"

"It's a long story."

He consults his watch. "I have time now. Please explain."

"Well…"

Chapter 36

"Mr. Controlling strikes again!" ~ Dakota

A FEW WEEKS LATER

Dakota

I glare at my bank statement. I want to say what I'm seeing – the return of my latest loan payment – makes no sense. But I know exactly what happened and I know exactly who to blame.

"Dakota," Rhett hollers as he knocks on the door to my suite.

I yank the door open. "How dare you?"

He holds up his hands. "Dare I what?"

"Don't give me your innocent act." I shake the bank statement at him. "I have all the proof I need right here."

He guides me inside before shutting the door behind us.

"Don't push me around!"

He blows out a breath. "I thought you'd prefer to discuss the issue in private."

He's right, but I'm not admitting anything. Not when he did what he did. "How dare you?"

He snatches the bank statement from my hand and throws it onto the kitchen counter before grasping my hand and hauling me near. I try to fight him but he's having none of it. He wraps his arms around me and holds me tight.

"Havoc, you can't expect me to allow the woman I love to be in debt to a loan shark."

I ignore how squishy I feel at his easy admission of his love for me and concentrate on the issue at hand. "Allow me?"

"Fuck," he mutters. "Wrong choice of words."

"No." I shove his shoulders but he doesn't budge. "I think you used the exact word you meant. You can't control me, Rhett. Look what happened when Adam controlled me. I ended up with a bunch of debt."

He growls. "Do not compare me to Adam. I don't want to control you. I want you to be free. Free of debt to do whatever you want."

I'd love to be free. "But this was my problem to deal with."

He growls as he pinches my chin. "No, it wasn't. It was your asshole husband's problem and you got stuck with it when he died."

If only I'd figured out what Adam was up to before he died. I purse my lips. "He was my husband. The law says I'm responsible for his debts."

"Really?" He cocks an eyebrow. "You're pulling the law as your trump card? You know damn well the debts to a loan shark are illegal as hell."

"Do I need to remind you of the snake?" I shiver.

He releases me and retreats a step. "I've changed my mind. Be mad at me all you want. We'll get through it. What I won't get through is watching you work yourself to death to pay off a debt that isn't yours to begin with."

"I was managing."

"Havoc." He sighs. "You've barely managed to pay the interest on the loan each month, and you're working two jobs. One of which I know pays extremely well."

"Extremely well? Are you saying I'm not worth it?"

"You're determined to fight me today."

I throw my arms in the air. "Of course, I am. You paid off my debt without my permission."

He stalks toward me. I try to hold my ground but I fail and end up retreating until my back hits the wall. He slams his hands next to my head.

"I want you to live with me."

"I know." He's told me often enough.

"But you refuse to move out of this ratty old motel suite as long as you're working the night shift here."

"The suite is part of my compensation. If I move out, Sadie can't afford to keep me on. And I can't lose this job."

"Your debt is paid. You don't need this job anymore."

I narrow my eyes on him. "I didn't ask you to save me."

"Havoc, you don't have to ask. Anything you need, I'll bleed to give you."

My body melts at his words. But I refuse to give in. I can't. He doesn't know everything.

"I want to give you a home, a family."

"You've given me a family," I whisper.

The Raider family has embraced me with open arms. They message and call, and pester me constantly. Rhett thinks they're cockblockers. I think they're wonderful.

He cups my face. "Let me give you a home, Havoc. Please."

I wish he could give me a home, but I'm afraid he won't want a home with me when he knows.

"I'll get you a pet. But not an otter." He shivers. "Otters freak me out."

I giggle. "Viking is adorable."

"She scurries on the floor." He smiles down at me and those blue eyes sparkle with warmth. "Move in with me and we'll get a dog."

The temptation is nearly too much to resist. I love dogs. I love him. I glance away before I give in to those pleading, piercing blue eyes.

"There's another problem," I mutter.

"Whatever it is, we'll deal with it together."

I nearly smile. How Rhett has changed his tune over the past weeks. He's gone from jumping to accuse me of keeping secrets to being ready to slay my dragons for me. And with all of his intensity focused on me, it's hard to resist him.

"We haven't discussed children." I whisper the words, hoping he won't hear me, but he does.

"I've been waiting for you to bring up this topic."

I scowl at him. I've been terrified to bring up the topic. Scared he'd leave me when he finds out the truth. And here he's been waiting for me to bring it up!

"You have? Why didn't you bring it up?"

"I didn't want to push you."

I lift a brow. "Didn't want to push me? But you'll pay my debts?"

"Two different things," he grumbles.

He really needs to stop being right. It's beyond annoying.

He kisses my forehead before grasping my hand and leading me to the sofa. He sits down and pulls me onto his lap until I'm straddling him.

"Children," he prompts once I'm settled.

I wring my hands together. "I don't want to have any."

"Don't want to give birth to any children or not have any?"

Leave it to Rhett to catch on to the distinction immediately. I debate stalling more, but my time is up. I have no excuses left.

"I don't want to give birth to any children."

"Because of your diabetes?"

I nod.

"Okay." He immediately gives in and I wait for the catch. "We'll adopt." And there it is.

"Who says I want to adopt?"

He tips his head back and barks out a laugh. He laughs with such vigor, his entire body shakes. He wipes the tears from his eyes when he finally calms down.

"What's so funny?"

"You." He chuckles. "Thinking, I don't know you."

I glare at him. "You don't know every little thing about me."

He pinches my chin and forces me to meet his gaze. "You, Dakota Bell Raider, want children. You want a family. It's your biggest desire. The one you're most afraid to reach for."

"First of all, my name is Dakota Bell."

"For now," he mutters.

I ignore him. I have enough problems. I don't need to add dealing with my feelings – which are frankly all over the place – about marrying him to the mix.

"Second, maybe my biggest desire is to kick you in the balls and watch you suffer."

He smirks. "But then I couldn't make you come with my cock."

I feel him begin to harden beneath me and my panties dampen in response. My body is easy for this man.

"Now." He presses his cock against my core and I nearly moan. "Are you going to admit you want a family? Or do I have to force the confession from you?"

"Force?"

"By not letting you come until you admit the truth."

I glare at him. "Orgasm denial doesn't sound fun."

"Oh, Havoc, it'll be fun. Trust me."

I debate giving in. Sex with Rhett is out of this world. But if I give in now, I don't know if I'll get the courage to say the words I need to say again.

"But don't you want children of your own?" I blurt out.

"Adopted children are still children of our own. I don't give a shit if the kid has my DNA or not. Dad proved to me, sharing

DNA does not make you a parent. And Stuart showed me you can be a parent without sharing DNA."

"How do you know the perfect thing to say to me?"

He smiles. "Because you were made for me. No one else could break through my walls the way you did." He grasps my hand and places it over his heart. "You and I are entwined. Two souls separated at birth but now reunited."

"When did you become this romantic?"

"Since the second I saw a gorgeous woman with curly, blonde hair sleeping in her car in the parking lot of the distillery."

"Which is why you yelled at me for being a vagrant and threatened to call the cops on me."

"You scared the hell out of me. One look at you and I knew you were going to change my life."

I grin. "But in a good way."

"In the best way."

"Agreed. I love you, Rhett."

"And I love you, Havoc." He trails kisses along my jaw. I tilt my neck to give him better access. He reaches my ear and bites the lobe. I moan.

"You gonna move in with me?" he whispers.

I give in. How can I not? "Yes."

"You gonna make a family with me?"

"Yes."

"I love you, Dakota. Down to my bones." He stands with me in his arms. "The heavy is done. Time to show you how much I love you."

"With orgasms, I hope."

He chuckles. "As many as you want for the rest of your life."

About the author

D.E. Haggerty is an American who has spent the majority of her adult life abroad. She has lived in Istanbul, various places throughout Germany, and currently finds herself in The Hague. She has been a military policewoman, a lawyer, a B&B owner/operator and now a writer.

Printed in Dunstable, United Kingdom